THIRD EDITION

3

Skills for Success
LISTENING AND SPEAKING

Margaret Brooks

198 Madison Avenue
New York, NY 10016 USA

Great Clarendon Street, Oxford, OX2 6DP, United Kingdom

Oxford University Press is a department of the University of Oxford.
It furthers the University's objective of excellence in research, scholarship,
and education by publishing worldwide. Oxford is a registered trade
mark of Oxford University Press in the UK and in certain other countries

© Oxford University Press 2020

The moral rights of the author have been asserted

First published in 2020

2024 2023 2022 2021 2020
10 9 8 7 6 5 4 3 2 1

No unauthorized photocopying

All rights reserved. No part of this publication may be reproduced, stored
in a retrieval system, or transmitted, in any form or by any means, without
the prior permission in writing of Oxford University Press, or as expressly
permitted by law, by licence or under terms agreed with the appropriate
reprographics rights organization. Enquiries concerning reproduction
outside the scope of the above should be sent to the ELT Rights
Department, Oxford University Press, at the address above

You must not circulate this work in any other form and you must impose
this same condition on any acquirer

Links to third party websites are provided by Oxford in good faith and for
information only. Oxford disclaims any responsibility for the materials
contained in any third party website referenced in this work

ISBN: 978 0 19 490496 4   STUDENT BOOK 2B WITH IQ ONLINE PACK
ISBN: 978 0 19 490484 1   STUDENT BOOK 2B AS PACK COMPONENT
ISBN: 978 0 19 490538 1   IQ ONLINE STUDENT WEBSITE

Printed in China

This book is printed on paper from certified and well-managed sources

ACKNOWLEDGMENTS

Back cover photograph: Oxford University Press building/David Fisher
Illustration by: p. 26 Karen Minor

The Publishers would like to thank the following for their kind permission to reproduce photographs and other copyright material: **123RF:** pp. 44 (log house/Benoit Daoust), (Gaudi house/Aliaksandr Mazurkevich), 50 (road rage/Antonio Diaz), 89 (friends interacting during meal/Mark Bowden), 141 (yurt/Gilad Fiskus), 154 (coastline/bloodua); **Alamy:** pp. 12 (bookshop café/Luis Dafos), 13 (booksigning/Jeff Morgan 08), 16 (wearing same shoes/Glasshouse Images), 18 (cyclist in city traffic/Scott Hortop Travel), 28 (cryptic frog/Dave and Sigrun Tollerton), 33 (colourful building/Maria Galan), 34 (house in Asir/ERIC LAFFORGUE), 37 (white living room/Jodie Johnson), 38 (red fire truck/imageBROKER), 52 (crowded bus/Torontonian), 58 (adults talking on balcony/Hero Images Inc.), 62 (Franklin Roosevelt/From Original Negative), (John Kennedy/Trinity Mirror /Mirrorpix), 76 (interacting with digital assistant/Image navi - QxQ images), 77 (GPS in car/age fotostock), 79 (1920s miners cottages/Allan Cash Picture Library), 93 (two sets of identical twins/Image Source Plus), 94 (male identical twins/Esther Moreno), 98 (multigenerational family/Kirn Vintage Stock), 116 (adult playing video game/ZUMA Press, Inc.), 123 (chess trophy/Kirn Vintage Stock), 146 (nomad family/Lucy Calder), 162 (irrigation sprinklers/Mauritius images GmbH), 165 (children carrying water/Jake Lyell), 168 (washing hands/Cultura Creative (RF)), 169 (indoor play area/Piotr Adamowicz), 171 (stomachache/Panther Media GmbH); **Getty:** pp. cover (Green color tile pattern/Fabian Krause/EyeEm), 4 (pet rocks/Al Freni), 5 (foot boats/Keystone/Stringer), 6 (old lightbulb/Science & Society Picture Library), 9 (organic vegetables/DOUGBERRY), 11 (bookshop/whitemay), 14 (Kente fabric weaving/Education Images), 23 (young women shopping/Peter Cade), 24 (chameleon/Juan Buitrago), 31 (bowerbird/Education Images), 37 (colourful living room/irina88w), 46 (helping elderly woman/SolStock), 48 (work colleagues heated discussion/praetorianphoto), 56 (attentive student classroom/skynesher), 67 (family meal/Ken Seet/Corbis/VCG), 68 (playing board games/Hero Images Inc.), 71 (man on laptop/supersizer), 75 (Tanja Hollander/Portland Press Herald), 83 (woman looking sad/EXTREME-PHOTOGRAPHER), 90 (large family photo/Amrish Saini/EyeEm), 96 (female twins/serts), 105 (looking at photographic memories/Yevgen Timashov), 107 (mother and daughter with photo album/RapidEye), 111 (grandmother greeting daughter/Ariel Skelley), 112 (girls playing video game/DaniloAndjus), 117 (father and son playing video game/Tom Werner), 118 (improve coordination/Jgalione), 120 (children chess tournament/Hero Images), 121 (Students Play Chess/VCG/Contributor), 124 (chess tournament/VCG), 128 (game developers/AFP), 136 (family playing cricket/uniquely india), 137 (family playing card game/shapecharge), 138 (cottage in mountains/Pete Rowbottom), 149 (modern apartment/pawel. gaul), 155 (Bosco Verticale building/marcociannarel), 157 (television interview/vm), 159 (cave dwellings/Alex Lapuerta), 160 (street cleaner/by MedioTuerto), 169 (outdoor play area/Susanne Kronholm), 176 (shipwrecked man/Martin Barraud), 178 (cattle drinking from stream/Damian Davies), 183 (woman cleaning house/Tony Hutchings); **Newscom:** p. 34 (Luis Barragán home/Javier Lira/Notimex); **OUP:** pp. 70 (woman at telegraph/Shutterstock/Everett Collection), 99 (DNA/Shutterstock /zffoto), 121–122 (chess pieces/Shutterstock/Nilotic); **Shutterstock:** pp. 2 (queue for Apple store/Sascha Steinbach/EPA-EFE/Shutterstock), 7 (velocipede/Imfoto), (fidget spinner/Olga V Kulakova), 19 (frustrated businessman/Creativa Images), 27 (cat/osobystist), 28 (false leaf katydid/PeingjaiChiangmai), (poison dart frog/Brandon Alms), 30 (monarch butterfly/Kate Scott), (zebras/The Maberhood), (coral snake/Mark_Kostich), (arctic fox in summer/COULANGES), (arctic fox in winter/JoannaPerchaluk), 40 (red jacket/Neamov), (red shoes/Chiyacat), 44 (modern city apartment/Trong Nguyen), (trailer home/Lowphoto), 51 (radio interview/antoniodiaz), 55 (disruptive students/Proshkin Aleksandr), 72 (woman using social media/Rawpixel.com), 86 (man gesturing confused/PicMy), 92 (left family portrait/Monkey Business Images), (right family portrait/Asia Images Group), 108 (two people talking/yurakrasil), 114 (Monopoly board/enchanted_fairy), 115 (Scrabble/Wachiwit), 118 (reduce stress/Aquarius Studio), (use as a learning tool/Rawpixel.com), (practice skills/Gorodenkoff), 125 (students on computers/mofaez), 126 (Simcity game/Pe3k), (phone screen/Stanisic Vladimir), 127 (adults playing board game/Standret), 130 (adults playing charades/Syda Productions), 132 (bowling/Corepics VOF), 133 (hide and seek/Iakov Filimonov), 140 (goats/Travel Pass Photos), 142 (wolf/Alexandr Kucheryavko), 143 (nomad herding livestock/CW Pix), 147 (high rise apartments/Naeblys), 149 (woman looking out of window/shurkin_son), 156 (person in Antarctica/Marcelo Alex), 158 (futuristic settlement on mars/ustas7777777), 164 (dry river bed/Peter Turner Photography), 170 (hand sanitizer/Elizaveta Galitckaia), 171 (cold/aslysun), 180 (water depth gauges/prajit48), 181 (wall sanitizer/Alexander Oganezov); **Third party:** p. 114 (Landlord's game/Thomas E Forsyth).

ACKNOWLEDGMENTS

We would like to acknowledge the teachers from all over the world who participated in the development process and review of *Q: Skills for Success* Third Edition.

USA

Kate Austin, Avila University, MO; **Sydney Bassett**, Auburn Global University, AL; **Michael Beamer**, USC, CA; **Renae Betten**, CBU, CA; **Pepper Boyer**, Auburn Global University, AL; **Marina Broeder**, Mission College, CA; **Thomas Brynmore**, Auburn Global University, AL; **Britta Burton**, Mission College, CA; **Kathleen Castello**, Mission College, CA; **Teresa Cheung**, North Shore Community College, MA; **Shantall Colebrooke**, Auburn Global University, AL; **Kyle Cooper**, Troy University, AL; **Elizabeth Cox**, Auburn Global University, AL; **Ashley Ekers**, Auburn Global University, AL; **Rhonda Farley**, Los Rios Community College, CA; **Marcus Frame**, Troy University, AL; **Lora Glaser**, Mission College, CA; **Hala Hamka**, Henry Ford College, MI; **Shelley A. Harrington**, Henry Ford College, MI; **Barrett J. Heusch**, Troy University, AL; **Beth Hill**, St. Charles Community College, MO; **Patty Jones**, Troy University, AL; **Tom Justice**, North Shore Community College, MA; **Robert Klein**, Troy University, AL; **Patrick Maestas**, Auburn Global University, AL; **Elizabeth Merchant**, Auburn Global University, AL; **Rosemary Miketa**, Henry Ford College, MI; **Myo Myint**, Mission College, CA; **Lance Noe**, Troy University, AL; **Irene Pannatier**, Auburn Global University, AL; **Annie Percy**, Troy University, AL; **Erin Robinson**, Troy University, AL; **Juliane Rosner**, Mission College, CA; **Mary Stevens**, North Shore Community College, MA; **Pamela Stewart**, Henry Ford College, MI; **Karen Tucker**, Georgia Tech, GA; **Loreley Wheeler**, North Shore Community College, MA; **Amanda Wilcox**, Auburn Global University, AL; **Heike Williams**, Auburn Global University, AL

Canada

Angelika Brunel, Collège Ahuntsic, QC; **David Butler**, English Language Institute, BC; **Paul Edwards**, Kwantlen Polytechnic University, BC; **Cody Hawver**, University of British Columbia, BC; **Olivera Jovovic**, Kwantlen Polytechnic University, BC; **Tami Moffatt**, University of British Columbia, BC; **Dana Pynn**, Vancouver Island University, BC

Latin America

Georgette Barreda, SENATI, Peru; **Claudia Cecilia Díaz Romero**, Colegio América, Mexico; **Jeferson Ferro**, Uninter, Brazil; **Mayda Hernández**, English Center, Mexico; **Jose Ixtaccihusatl**, Instituto Tecnológico de Tecomatlán, Mexico; **Andreas Paulus Pabst**, CBA Idiomas, Brazil; **Amanda Carla Pas**, Instituição de Ensino Santa Izildinha, Brazil; **Allen Quesada Pacheco**, University of Costa Rica, Costa Rica; **Rolando Sánchez**, Escuela Normal de Tecámac, Mexico; **Luis Vasquez**, CESNO, Mexico

Asia

Asami Atsuko, Jissen Women's University, Japan; **Rene Bouchard**, Chinzei Keiai Gakuen, Japan; **Francis Brannen**, Sangmyung University, South Korea; **Haeyun Cho**, Sogang University, South Korea; **Daniel Craig**, Sangmyung University, South Korea; **Thomas Cuming**, Royal Melbourne Institute of Technology, Vietnam; **Nguyen Duc Dat**, OISP, Vietnam; **Wayne Devitte**, Tokai University, Japan; **James D. Dunn**, Tokai University, Japan; **Fergus Hann**, Tokai University, Japan; **Michael Hood**, Nihon University College of Commerce, Japan; **Hideyuki Kashimoto**, Shijonawate High School, Japan; **David Kennedy**, Nihon University, Japan; **Anna Youngna Kim**, Sogang University, South Korea; **Jae Phil Kim**, Sogang University, South Korea; **Jaganathan Krishnasamy**, GB Academy, Malaysia; **Peter Laver**, Incheon National University, South Korea; **Hung Hoang Le**, Ho Chi Minh City University of Technology, Vietnam; **Hyon Sook Lee**, Sogang University, South Korea; **Ji-seon Lee**, Iruda English Institute, South Korea; **Joo Young Lee**, Sogang University, South Korea; **Phung Tu Luc**, Ho Chi Minh City University of Technology, Vietnam; **Richard Mansbridge**, Hoa Sen University, Vietnam; **Kahoko Matsumoto**, Tokai University, Japan; **Elizabeth May**, Sangmyung University, South Korea; **Naoyuki Naganuma**, Tokai University, Japan; **Hiroko Nishikage**, Taisho University, Japan; **Yongjun Park**, Sangji University, South Korea; **Paul Rogers**, Dongguk University, South Korea; **Scott Schafer**, Inha University, South Korea; **Michael Schvaudner**, Tokai University, Japan; **Brendan Smith**, RMIT University, School of Languages and English, Vietnam; **Peter Snashall**, Huachiew Chalermprakiet University, Thailand; **Makoto Takeda**, Sendai Third Senior High School, Japan; **Peter Talley**, Mahidol University, Faculty of ICT, Thailand; **Byron Thigpen**, Sogang University, South Korea; **Junko Yamaai**, Tokai University, Japan; **Junji Yamada**, Taisho University, Japan; **Sayoko Yamashita**, Jissen Women's University, Japan; **Masami Yukimori**, Taisho University, Japan

Middle East and North Africa

Sajjad Ahmad, Taibah University, Saudi Arabia; **Basma Alansari**, Taibah University, Saudi Arabia; **Marwa Al-ashqar**, Taibah University, Saudi Arabia; **Dr. Rashid Al-Khawaldeh**, Taibah University, Saudi Arabia; **Mohamed Almohamed**, Taibah University, Saudi Arabia; **Dr Musaad Alrahaili**, Taibah University, Saudi Arabia; **Hala Al Sammar**, Kuwait University, Kuwait; **Ahmed Alshammari**, Taibah University, Saudi Arabia; **Ahmed Alshamy**, Taibah University, Saudi Arabia; **Doniazad sultan AlShraideh**, Taibah University, Saudi Arabia; **Sahar Amer**, Taibah University, Saudi Arabia; **Nabeela Azam**, Taibah University, Saudi Arabia; **Hassan Bashir**, Edex, Saudi Arabia; **Rachel Batchilder**, College of the North Atlantic, Qatar; **Nicole Cuddie**, Community College of Qatar, Qatar; **Mahdi Duris**, King Saud University, Saudi Arabia; **Ahmed Ege**, Institute of Public Administration, Saudi Arabia; **Magda Fadle**, Victoria College, Egypt; **Mohammed Hassan**, Taibah University, Saudi Arabia; **Tom Hodgson**, Community College of Qatar, Qatar; **Ayub Agbar Khan**, Taibah University, Saudi Arabia; **Cynthia Le Joncour**, Taibah University, Saudi Arabia; **Ruari Alexander MacLeod**, Community College of Qatar, Qatar; **Nasir Mahmood**, Taibah University, Saudi Arabia; **Duria Salih Mahmoud**, Taibah University, Saudi Arabia; **Ameera McKoy**, Taibah University, Saudi Arabia; **Chaker Mhamdi**, Buraimi University College, Oman; **Baraa Shiekh Mohamed**, Community College of Qatar, Qatar; **Abduleelah Mohammed**, Taibah University, Saudi Arabia; **Shumaila Nasir**, Taibah University, Saudi Arabia; **Kevin Onwordi**, Taibah University, Saudi Arabia; **Dr. Navid Rahmani**, Community College of Qatar, Qatar; **Dr. Sabah Salman Sabbah**, Community College of Qatar, Qatar; **Salih**, Taibah University, Saudi Arabia; **Verna Santos-Nafrada**, King Saud University, Saudi Arabia; **Gamal Abdelfattah Shehata**, Taibah University, Saudi Arabia; **Ron Stefan**, Institute of Public Administration, Saudi Arabia; **Dr. Saad Torki**, Imam Abdulrahman Bin Faisal University, Dammam, Saudi Arabia; **Silvia Yafai**, Applied Technology High School/Secondary Technical School, UAE; **Mahmood Zar**, Taibah University, Saudi Arabia; **Thouraya Zheni**, Taibah University, Saudi Arabia

Turkey

Sema Babacan, Istanbul Medipol University; **Bilge Çöllüoğlu Yakar**, Bilkent University; **Liana Corniel**, Koc University; **Savas Geylanioglu**, Izmir Bahcesehir Science and Technology College; **Öznur Güler**, Giresun University; **Selen Bilginer Halefoğlu**, Maltepe University; **Ahmet Konukoğlu**, Hasan Kalyoncu University; **Mehmet Salih Yoğun**, Gaziantep Hasan Kalyoncu University; **Fatih Yücel**, Beykent University

Europe

Amina Al Hashamia, University of Exeter, UK; **Irina Gerasimova**, Saint-Petersburg Mining University, Russia; **Jodi**, Las Dominicas, Spain; **Marina Khanykova**, School 179, Russia; **Oksana Postnikova**, Lingua Practica, Russia; **Nina Vasilchenko**, Soho-Bridge Language School, Russia

Q: Skills for Success THIRD EDITION

CRITICAL THINKING

The unique critical thinking approach of the *Q: Skills for Success* series has been further enhanced in the Third Edition. New features help you analyze, synthesize, and develop your ideas.

Unit question
The thought-provoking unit questions engage you with the topic and provide a critical thinking framework for the unit.

UNIT QUESTION
How can colors be useful?

A. Discuss these questions with your classmates.
1. Why can wearing dark clothes at night be dangerous? Why do traffic police in some countries wear orange?
2. Imagine you want to paint your house. What color do you choose? Why?
3. Look at the photo. How is color useful to this animal?

Analysis
You can discuss your opinion of each listening text and analyze how it changes your perspective on the unit question.

SAY WHAT YOU THINK
SYNTHESIZE Think about the unit video, Listening 1, and Listening 2 as you discuss the questions.
1. Many families in the world today have family members who live in different countries. How does this affect family life? What are the advantages and disadvantages?
2. How important is it to keep in touch with your larger family, that is aunts, uncles, cousins, grandparents, and so on?
3. Who has been an important person in your life? It might be a family member or other person. Why is the person important?

NEW! Critical Thinking Strategy with video
Each unit includes a Critical Thinking Strategy with activities to give you step-by-step guidance in critical analysis of texts. An accompanying instructional video (available on iQ Online) provides extra support and examples.

NEW! Bloom's Taxonomy
Pink activity headings integrate verbs from Bloom's Taxonomy to help you see how each activity develops critical thinking skills.

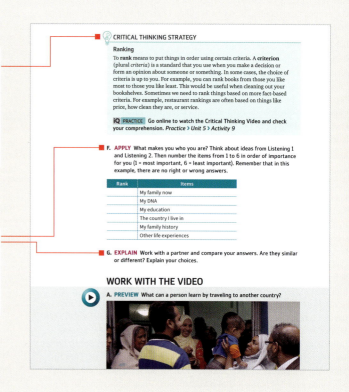

iv

THREE TYPES OF VIDEO

UNIT VIDEO

The unit videos include high-interest documentaries and reports on a wide variety of subjects, all linked to the unit topic and question.

NEW! "Work with the Video" pages guide you in watching, understanding, and discussing the unit videos. The activities help you see the connection to the Unit Question and the other texts in the unit.

NEW! In some units, one of the main listening texts is a video.

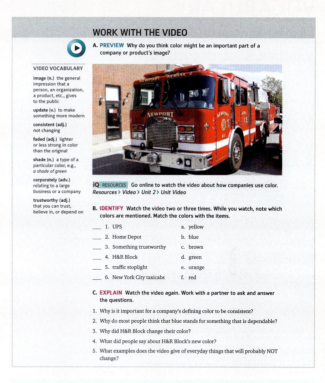

CRITICAL THINKING VIDEO

NEW! Narrated by the *Q* series authors, these short videos give you further instruction on the Critical Thinking Strategy of each unit using engaging images and graphics. You can use them to gain a deeper understanding of the Critical Thinking Strategy.

SKILLS VIDEO

NEW! These instructional videos provide illustrated explanations of skills and grammar points in the Student Book. They can be viewed in class or assigned for a flipped classroom, for homework, or for review. One skill video is available for every unit.

Easily access all videos in the Resources section of iQ Online.

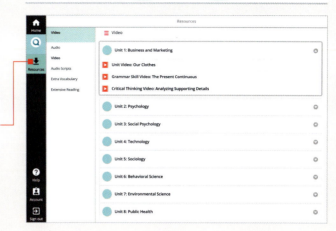

VOCABULARY

A research-based vocabulary program focuses on the words you need to know academically and professionally.

The vocabulary syllabus in *Q: Skills for Success* is correlated to the CEFR (see page 184) and linked to two word lists: the Oxford 3000 and the OPAL (Oxford Phrasal Academic Lexicon).

🔑 OXFORD 3000

The Oxford 3000 lists the core words that every learner at the A1–B2 level needs to know. Items in the word list are selected for their frequency and usefulness from the Oxford English Corpus (a database of over 2 billion words).

Vocabulary Key
In vocabulary activities, 🔑 shows you the word is in the Oxford 3000 and **OPAL** shows you the word or phrase is in the OPAL.

PREVIEW THE LISTENING

A. VOCABULARY Here are some words and phrases from Listening 2. Read the definitions. Then complete each sentence with the correct word or phrase.

> **attentive** *(adjective)* watching or listening carefully
> **courteous** *(adjective)* polite, having courtesy
> **deal with** *(verb phrase)* to solve a problem
> **improve** *(verb)* 🔑 OPAL to make something better
> **influence** *(noun)* 🔑 OPAL the power to change how someone or something acts
> **principal** *(noun)* the person in charge of a school
> **respect** *(noun)* 🔑 OPAL consideration for the rights and feelings of other people
> **shout out** *(verb phrase)* to say something in a loud voice
> **valuable** *(adjective)* 🔑 OPAL very useful or important

🔑 Oxford 3000™ words   **OPAL** Oxford Phrasal Academic Lexicon

1. I apologized to show Sue I have _____ for her feelings.
2. The parents are meeting with the _____ tonight to discuss problems at school. She can make new school rules to stop the problems.

OPAL
OXFORD PHRASAL ACADEMIC LEXICON

NEW! The OPAL is a collection of four word lists that provide an essential guide to the most important words and phrases to know for academic English. The word lists are based on the Oxford Corpus of Academic English and the British Academic Spoken English corpus. The OPAL includes both spoken and written academic English and both individual words and longer phrases.

Academic Language tips in the Student Book give information about how words and phrases from the OPAL are used and offer help with features such as collocations and phrases.

ACADEMIC LANGUAGE
The word *relationship* is often used in academic contexts. Notice that the suffix *-ship* is also used in the noun *friendship*. The suffix *-ship* indicates a state or condition.

_____ | **OPAL**
Oxford Phrasal Academic Lexicon

3. We need curtains on those windows. Without them, we have no _____ in the bedroom.
4. It is hard to discuss some things online. You need a _____ conversation where you can see the other person.
5. His _____ with Tom is very important to Reza. They have known each other for many years.
6. The newspaper _____ said that there will be bad snowstorms in the Midwest today.
7. Their family has lived here _____. I mean a very long time, more than 100 years.
8. The lecturer made some very _____ statements about social media. It gave me a lot to think about.

iQ PRACTICE Go online for more practice with the vocabulary.
Practice > Unit 4 > Activities 3–4

B. PREVIEW You are going to listen to a lecture about social media and friendship. Work with a partner. List one good thing and one possible problem related to social media and friendships.

WORK WITH THE LISTENING

🎧 **A. LISTEN AND TAKE NOTES** Listen to Part 1 of the lecture. The speaker mentions three points that will be in the lecture. Prepare a piece of paper to take notes. List the three points and leave space for writing after each one.

EXTENSIVE READING

NEW! Extensive Reading is a program of reading for pleasure at a level that matches your language ability.

There are many benefits to Extensive Reading:

- It helps you to become a better reader in general.
- It helps to increase your reading speed.
- It can improve your reading comprehension.
- It increases your vocabulary range.
- It can help you improve your grammar and writing skills.
- It's great for motivation to read something that is interesting for its own sake.

Each unit of *Q: Skills for Success* Third Edition has been aligned to an Oxford Graded Reader based on the appropriate topic and level of language proficiency. The first chapter of each recommended graded reader can be downloaded from iQ Online Resources.

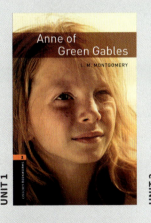
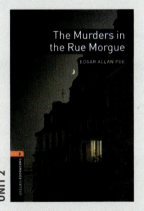

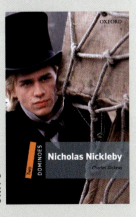
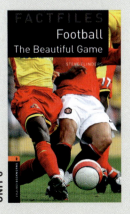

What is iQ ONLINE?

iQ ONLINE extends your learning beyond the classroom.

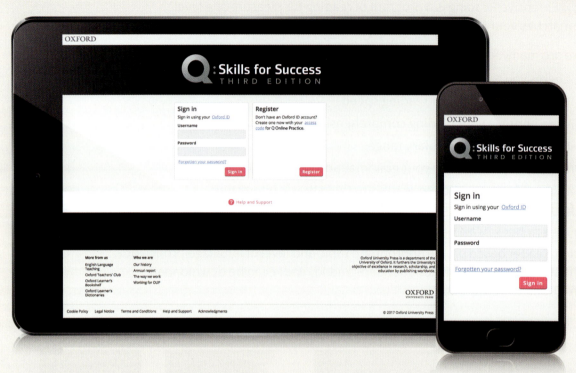

- Practice activities provide essential skills practice and support.
- Automatic grading and progress reports show you what you have mastered and where you need more practice.
- The Discussion Board allows you to discuss the Unit Questions and helps you develop your critical thinking.
- Essential resources such as audio and video are easy to access anytime.

NEW TO THE THIRD EDITION

- iQ Online is optimized for mobile use so you can use it on your phone.
- An updated interface allows easy navigation around the activities, tests, resources, and scores.
- New Critical Thinking Videos expand on the Critical Thinking Strategies in the Student Book.
- The Extensive Reading program helps you improve your vocabulary and reading skills.

How to use iQ ONLINE

Go to **Practice** to find additional practice and support to complement your learning in the classroom.

Go to **Resources** to find:
- All Student Book video
- All Student Book audio
- Critical Thinking videos
- Skills videos
- Extensive Reading

Go to **Messages** and **Discussion Board** to communicate with your teacher and classmates.

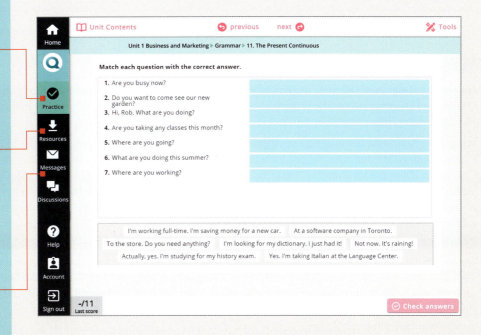

A progress bar shows you how many activities you have completed.

View your scores for all activities.

Online tests assigned by your teacher help you assess your progress and see where you need more practice.

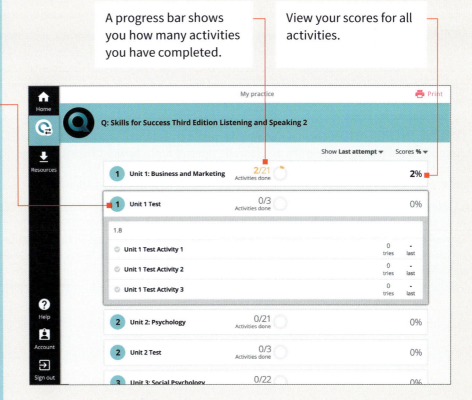

AUTHOR AND CONSULTANTS

AUTHOR

Margaret Brooks worked for many years as a teacher and administrator in a variety of English language-teaching programs in the Dominican Republic and Costa Rica, including serving as a professor at the Autonomous University of Santo Domingo and working with a private company to develop specialized language courses for businesses in Costa Rica. She has also written and developed course material for a wide range of ELT programs.

SERIES CONSULTANTS

Lawrence J. Zwier holds an M.A. in TESL from the University of Minnesota. He is currently the Associate Director for Curriculum Development at the English Language Center at Michigan State University in East Lansing. He has taught ESL/EFL in the United States, Saudi Arabia, Malaysia, Japan, and Singapore.

Marguerite Ann Snow holds a Ph.D. in Applied Linguistics from UCLA. She teaches in the TESOL M.A. program in the Charter College of Education at California State University, Los Angeles. She was a Fulbright scholar in Hong Kong and Cyprus. In 2006, she received the President's Distinguished Professor award at CSULA. She has trained ESL teachers in the United States and EFL teachers in more than 25 countries. She is the author/editor of numerous publications in the areas of content-based instruction, English for academic purposes, and standards for English teaching and learning. She is a co-editor of *Teaching English as a Second or Foreign Language* (4th ed.).

CRITICAL THINKING CONSULTANT **James Dunn** is a Junior Associate Professor at Tokai University and the Coordinator of the JALT Critical Thinking Special Interest Group. His research interests include critical thinking skills' impact on student brain function during English learning as measured by EEG. His educational goals are to help students understand that they are capable of more than they might think and to expand their cultural competence with critical thinking and higher-order thinking skills.

ASSESSMENT CONSULTANT **Elaine Boyd** has worked in assessment for over 30 years for international testing organizations. She has designed and delivered courses in assessment literacy and is also the author of several EL exam coursebooks for leading publishers. She is an Associate Tutor (M.A. TESOL/Linguistics) at University College, London. Her research interests are classroom assessment, issues in managing feedback, and intercultural competences.

VOCABULARY CONSULTANT **Cheryl Boyd Zimmerman** is Professor Emeritus at California State University, Fullerton. She specialized in second-language vocabulary acquisition, an area in which she is widely published. She taught graduate courses on second-language acquisition, culture, vocabulary, and the fundamentals of TESOL, and has been a frequent invited speaker on topics related to vocabulary teaching and learning. She is the author of *Word Knowledge: A Vocabulary Teacher's Handbook* and Series Director of *Inside Reading, Inside Writing,* and *Inside Listening and Speaking,* published by Oxford University Press.

ONLINE INTEGRATION **Chantal Hemmi** holds an Ed.D. TEFL and is a Japan-based teacher trainer and curriculum designer. Since leaving her position as Academic Director of the British Council in Tokyo, she has been teaching at the Center for Language Education and Research at Sophia University in an EAP/CLIL program offered for undergraduates. She delivers lectures and teacher trainings throughout Japan, Indonesia, and Malaysia.

COMMUNICATIVE GRAMMAR CONSULTANT **Nancy Schoenfeld** holds an M.A. in TESOL from Biola University in La Mirada, California, and has been an English language instructor since 2000. She has taught ESL in California and Hawaii and EFL in Thailand and Kuwait. She has also trained teachers in the United States and Indonesia. Her interests include teaching vocabulary, extensive reading, and student motivation. She is currently an English Language Instructor at Kuwait University.

CONTENTS

Welcome to *Q: Skills for Success* Third Edition iv
What is iQ Online? viii
Author and Consultants x

UNIT 5 Sociology – What does it mean to be part of a family? **90**
    Note-taking Skill: Using a simple outline 92
    Listening 1: Twins in the Family 93
    Listening Skill: Listening for reasons and explanations 97
    Listening 2: Family History 98
    Critical Thinking Strategy: Ranking 102
    Work with the Video: Nadiya's Family 102
    Vocabulary Skill: Word families: verbs, nouns, adjectives 104
    Grammar: Auxiliary verbs in questions 105
    Pronunciation: Intonation in questions with *or* 107
    Speaking Skill: Expressing opinions 108
    Unit Assignment: Give a short speech 109

UNIT 6 Behavioral Science – How can playing games be good for you? **112**
    Note-taking Skill: Reviewing and editing notes 114
    Listening Skill: Listening for dates and other numbers 115
    Listening 1: Why Should Adults Play Video Games? 116
    Listening 2: Chess Champions 120
    Critical Thinking Strategy: Identifying "false" inferences 124
    Work with the Video: Is Gaming the Future of Education? 125
    Vocabulary Skill: Word families: suffixes 127
    Grammar: Imperative verbs 129
    Pronunciation: Word stress 131
    Speaking Skill: Giving instructions 132
    Unit Assignment: Develop and present an idea for a new game 134

UNIT 7 Environmental Science – How do people survive in extreme environments? **138**
    Note-taking Skill: Preparing to take notes in class 140
    Listening 1 (Video): The Nomads of Outer Mongolia 141
    Critical Thinking Strategy: Categorizing 144
    Listening Skill: Recognizing a speaker's attitude 145
    Listening 2: High-Rise Living 147
    Vocabulary Skill: Compound nouns 150
    Grammar: Future with *will* 152
    Pronunciation: Word stress in compound nouns 153
    Speaking Skill: Summarizing 154
    Unit Assignment: Role-play an interview 156

UNIT 8 Public Health – How important is cleanliness? **160**
    Listening 1 (Video): Water for Life 162
    Listening Skill: Recognizing facts and opinions 166
    Note-taking Skill: Using notes to write a summary 167
    Listening 2: Is It Possible to Be Too Clean? 168
    Vocabulary Skill: Using the dictionary 172
    Grammar: *If* clauses for future possibility 174
    Pronunciation: Function words and stress 175
    Critical Thinking Strategy: Appraising solutions to problems 177
    Speaking Skill: Participating in a group discussion 179
    Unit Assignment: Give a persuasive presentation 180

Vocabulary List and CEFR Correlation 184

Sociology

NOTE-TAKING	using a simple outline
LISTENING	listening for reasons and explanations
CRITICAL THINKING	ranking
VOCABULARY	word families: verbs, nouns, adjectives
GRAMMAR	auxiliary verbs in questions
PRONUNCIATION	intonation in questions with *or*
SPEAKING	expressing opinions

UNIT QUESTION

What does it mean to be part of a family?

A. Discuss these questions with your classmates.

1. What is your definition of a family?
2. Which members of your family influence your life? How?
3. Look at the photo. Who do you think the people are?

B. Listen to *The Q Classroom* online. Then choose the correct phrases from the box to complete the sentences.

a. don't have good relationships
b. family has to come first
c. for these people, friends are their family
d. she always has her family
e. you aren't alone

1. Yuna says that being part of a family means that _d_ .
2. Marcus agrees with Yuna and says it also means that ___.
3. Sophy thinks being part of a family means that ___.
4. Felix says that some people ___ with family members.
5. Because of this, Felix says that ___.

iQ PRACTICE Go to the online discussion board to discuss the Unit Question with your classmates. *Practice > Unit 5 > Activity 1*

UNIT OBJECTIVE

Listen to an interview and a lecture. Gather information and ideas to give a speech about families.

NOTE-TAKING SKILL Using a simple outline

Using an outline is one way of keeping notes organized. You can make a simple outline based on questions and answers. Sometimes, a speaker will begin by stating the questions he or she will answer, as in this example.

> Today I'm going to talk about the family. What were families like in the past? How are families changing today? And finally, what will the family be like in the future?

In a case like this, you can make an outline by writing short notes about the questions and leaving space after each one to write notes about the speaker's comments.

The Family

A   the past

B   changes

C   the future

IDENTIFY Listen to the introduction to a talk about families around the world. Then make a simple question outline that you could use to take notes.

iQ PRACTICE Go online for more practice using a simple outline to take notes.
Practice > Unit 5 > Activity 2

UNIT 5   What does it mean to be part of a family?

LISTENING

LISTENING 1 Twins in the Family

OBJECTIVE ▶ You are going to listen to an interview with psychologist Dr. Mona Bashir. Dr. Bashir talks about twins and their life in the family. As you listen, gather information and ideas about what it means to be part of a family.

PREVIEW THE LISTENING

A. VOCABULARY Here are some words from Listening 1. Read the paragraphs. Then write each underlined word next to the correct definition.

My friends Layla and Manar are <u>twins</u>! They have exactly the same physical <u>appearance</u>. Their eyes, their hair, and even their noses look the same. Twins <u>inherit</u> the same hair and eye color from their parents. Sometimes twins even act very much alike. Layla and Manar live in different cities. Yesterday, they both went shopping for shoes. They both bought the same kind of shoes. They were the same color, style, and brand. That was an amazing <u>coincidence</u>. They didn't plan to buy the same shoes. It just happened!

1. _____ (*noun*) two things that happen at the same time by chance
2. _____ (*noun*) the way someone looks
3. _____ (*verb*) to get a characteristic from your parents
4. _____ (*noun*) two children born to the same mother at the same time

LISTENING 1 93

I am very close to my sister, Louise. We aren't twins, but I am only one year younger than she is. As children, we had a <u>tendency</u> to do everything together. When I was ready to go to college, I wanted to go to the same university as Louise. But our parents didn't agree with that idea. They felt we each needed to develop our own <u>identity</u>. Now Louise is married and has her own family. We have <u>separate</u> lives, but we still <u>get along</u> very well and enjoy doing things together.

5. _____ (*adjective*) different; not connected
6. _____ (*noun*) something a person usually does
7. _____ (*noun*) who or what a person or thing is
8. _____ (*verb phrase*) to have a friendly relationship with someone

iQ PRACTICE Go online for more practice with the vocabulary.
Practice > Unit 5 > Activities 3–4

B. PREVIEW You are going to listen to an interview about twins. What do you think psychologist Dr. Mona Bashir will say about twins? Circle your choice.

a. Twins should share everything and be in the same classes at school.

b. Twins need to be able to develop their own individual personalities.

WORK WITH THE LISTENING

A. LISTEN AND TAKE NOTES Listen to Part 1 of the interview. The interviewer asks Dr. Bashir some questions. Use a simple outline with question notes to take notes about the answers.

twins — What physical differences?

personalities? — Like same things or different?

How twins relate to family?

B. INVESTIGATE Listen to Part 2 of the interview. Again, the interviewer asks questions. Take notes about the questions and answers.

C. IDENTIFY Listen to the whole interview. Add more information to your notes. Then read the questions and choose the correct answers.

1. What does Dr. Bashir say about the differences and similarities between her twin boys?
    a. There are small differences in their appearance and personalities.
    b. Faris is very social and likes sports, but Fahad is quiet and likes music.
    c. There are no differences in their physical appearance.

2. How is the twins' relationship with their older brother different from their relationship with each other?
    a. They don't get along with their brother because they can't communicate.
    b. They can communicate with their brother by just looking at him.
    c. They get along with their brother, but their own relationship is closer.

3. What does the example of the Springer-Lewis twins show about twins raised in different families?
    a. They have problems later in life.
    b. They are very different from their families.
    c. They can be very similar to each other.

4. What conclusion does Dr. Bashir make based on this story and her own experience?
    a. Our personalities are formed by chance and have no connection to our family.
    b. Our personalities are formed by both inherited tendencies and family influence.
    c. Our personalities are formed by our life experiences. We don't inherit them.

D. RESTATE Answer the questions. Use your notes to help you. Then listen again and check your answers.

1. Which twin is taller, Faris or Fahad?

2. What sports do Faris and Fahad like to play?

3. How did the twins communicate when they were babies?

LISTENING 1 95

4. What did Dr. Bashir and her husband do when the boys started first grade?

5. Why did they do this?

6. How do Faris and Fahad feel when they are together?

7. What two things did both of the Springer-Lewis twins like?

8. What two small coincidences did Dr. Bashir mention in relation to the Springer-Lewis twins?

E. **EVALUATE** Do you think Dr. Bashir agrees or disagrees with these statements? Write *A* (agree) or *D* (disagree).

____ 1. It is a good idea for parents to dress twins in the same clothes.

____ 2. It is a good thing for twins to have different interests and friends sometimes.

____ 3. Twins often don't get along very well with other children in the family.

____ 4. Although they are similar in many ways, twins will usually have some differences in their appearance and personality.

____ 5. We are not born with any certain personality. Personality comes from our life experiences in the family and outside.

F. **EVALUATE** Work in a group. Compare your answers to Activity E. Then discuss the answers that are different.

iQ PRACTICE Go online for additional listening and comprehension.
Practice > Unit 5 > Activity 5

SAY WHAT YOU THINK

DISCUSS Discuss the questions in a group.

1. Which do you think has more influence on your personality: characteristics you inherit or people and events in your life? Why?
2. Think of the coincidences in the Springer-Lewis twins' lives. What are some coincidences among people you know?
3. Look at the photo of adult twins on page 96. How do you think they are different from each other as adults?

LISTENING SKILL Listening for reasons and explanations

Good speakers give **reasons** and **explanations** to support what they say. When you hear a speaker make a statement about something or express an opinion, it's important to ask yourself, "Why did the speaker say this?" Then listen for reasons or an explanation. Look at this example from "Twins in the Family."

Statement: Starting in the first grade, we decided to put them [the twins] in different classes in school.

Question to ask yourself: Why did they put the twins in different classes?

Reasons: They had different teachers and school friends. These experiences helped them develop their own personalities.

 A. EXPLAIN Listen to the interview again. Answer the questions.

TIP FOR SUCCESS
In a conversation, look at the person who is speaking. Focus on what the person is saying. You will understand more.

1. Why does Faris prefer to play soccer rather than tennis?

   _____

2. Why do the twins feel like different people when they are apart?

   _____

 B. IDENTIFY Listen to the radio call-in show. Complete the statements.

1. Hal probably feels closer to his friends than his family because _____

   _____

   _____

2. Marielena thinks family members are more critical than friends because

   _____

   _____

iQ PRACTICE Go online for more practice with listening for reasons and explanations. *Practice > Unit 5 > Activity 6*

LISTENING 2   Family History

OBJECTIVE ▶ You are going to listen to a lecturer describe how a group of famous African Americans used DNA to learn about their family history. As you listen, gather information and ideas about what it means to be part of a family.

PREVIEW THE LISTENING

VOCABULARY SKILL REVIEW

In Unit 1, you learned about noun + verb collocations. The noun *record* is often used with the verbs *check* and *destroy*, and one other verb. What verb is *record* used with in this activity?

A. VOCABULARY Here are some words from Listening 2. Read the sentences. Then choose the answer that best matches the meaning of each underlined word.

1. Our assignment is to <u>search</u> for information about where our grandparents were born. I'll go to the library, and you check online.

   a. look for

   b. write down

2. Evelyn's great-great-grandfather was a <u>slave</u> in Georgia. He ran away to Canada.

   a. a person who is free

   b. a person who is owned by another person

98   UNIT 5   What does it mean to be part of a family?

3. Our school library has an electronic <u>database</u> with the titles and authors of all of the books in the library. You can look at it online.

   a. a book of information

   b. information organized and stored in a computer

4. I am very close to my <u>cousin</u> Amal. I often see her when our families get together.

   a. the child of an aunt or uncle

   b. a very special friend

5. Some of Ron's <u>ancestors</u> on his mother's side of the family came from Italy in the 1880s.

   a. relatives who lived a long time ago

   b. aunts and uncles

6. We need <u>input</u> from everyone on the team. Adel, what do you think?

   a. ideas and information

   b. computer files

7. Alfredo was never an active <u>participant</u> in the class, so most students didn't like being in his group. He did not like to practice speaking.

   a. someone who teaches a class

   b. someone who takes part in something

8. The city keeps <u>records</u> of all the people who were born or died here. They file and keep track of them all.

   a. files of information

   b. disks with music on them

ACADEMIC LANGUAGE

The word *input* is often used in spoken and written academic English. It originally referred to data or information fed into computers. Now it also refers to contributions of ideas or information in any situation. *Kayla gave us valuable **input** during our discussion.*

OPAL
Oxford Phrasal Academic Lexicon

iQ PRACTICE Go online for more practice with the vocabulary.
Practice > Unit 5 > Activities 7–8

B. **PREVIEW** You are going to listen to a lecture about how a group of people used DNA to learn about their family history. Write two questions you would like to ask about your own family history.

1. _____

2. _____

LISTENING 2   99

WORK WITH THE LISTENING

A. LISTEN AND TAKE NOTES The speaker in this lecture often makes statements and then gives reasons and explanations to explain them. Listen and take notes about the explanations for these statements.

> Most African Americans have little information about their ancestors.
>
> Henry Louis Gates used DNA to study the history of African-American families.
>
> The results of Gates's study were surprising.
>
> Another person in Gates's study, author Bliss Broyard, had a different experience.

B. INVESTIGATE Work with a partner. Review and edit your notes. Then listen again and add more information.

C. EVALUATE Check (✓) the sentence that best states the main idea of the lecture.

____ 1. You need to know your family history to know who you really are.

____ 2. Our genes and our family history form part of our identity, but they don't tell the whole story.

____ 3. Some participants were surprised to discover how many of their ancestors came from places other than Africa.

D. IDENTIFY Read the questions. Choose the correct answers. Use your notes to help you. Then listen and check your answers.

1. What is one reason that some African Americans have little information about their family history?

    a. Their ancestors came to America as slaves.

    b. They weren't interested in family history.

    c. Their grandparents never told them family stories.

2. Who is Henry Louis Gates?

   a. a scientist

   b. a historian

   c. a journalist

3. What new tool did Henry Louis Gates use in his study of the African-Americans' families?

   a. newspaper stories

   b. books and public records

   c. DNA

4. What does it mean when two people have the same "markers" in their DNA?

   a. They are brothers or sisters.

   b. They are not related.

   c. They have a common ancestor.

5. Where did some of Henry Louis Gates's ancestors come from?

   a. Ireland

   b. Scotland

   c. England

6. What percentage of Bliss Broyard's DNA comes from her African ancestors?

   a. 15 percent

   b. 18 percent

   c. 50 percent

E. **APPLY** Work with a partner. Read the excerpt from Listening 2 and try to fill in the missing words. Then listen and check your answers.

Some people have little information about their _____.
                                                         1
For example, the ancestors of most African Americans came to America as

_____. There are very few _____ records of
        2   3

their family _____, especially before they came to America.
                   4

For this _____, historian Henry Louis Gates recently used
              5

_____ to study the family history of several famous African
     6

Americans. _____ in the study wanted to know what
                  7

_____ of Africa their families came from. Who were their
     8

African ancestors?

CRITICAL THINKING STRATEGY

Ranking

To **rank** means to put things in order using certain criteria. A **criterion** (plural *criteria*) is a standard that you use when you make a decision or form an opinion about someone or something. In some cases, the choice of criteria is up to you. For example, you can rank books from those you like most to those you like least. This would be useful when cleaning out your bookshelves. Sometimes we need to rank things based on more fact-based criteria. For example, restaurant rankings are often based on things like price, how clean they are, or service.

iQ PRACTICE Go online to watch the Critical Thinking Video and check your comprehension. *Practice > Unit 5 > Activity 9*

F. **APPLY** What makes you who you are? Think about ideas from Listening 1 and Listening 2. Then number the items from 1 to 6 in order of importance for you (1 = most important, 6 = least important). Remember that in this example, there are no right or wrong answers.

Rank	Items
	My family now
	My DNA
	My education
	The country I live in
	My family history
	Other life experiences

G. **EXPLAIN** Work with a partner and compare your answers. Are they similar or different? Explain your choices.

WORK WITH THE VIDEO

A. **PREVIEW** What can a person learn by traveling to another country?

iQ RESOURCES Go online to watch the video about a woman who travels to visit her family. *Resources > Video > Unit 5 > Unit Video*

VIDEO VOCABULARY

chef (n.) a person who works as the chief cook in a restaurant

knock (v.) to make a noise by hitting something

mutton (n.) the meat from an adult sheep

curry (n.) a dish with meat, vegetables, and many spices popular in India and other Asian countries

B. ANALYZE Watch the video again. Choose the correct answers.

1. How did Nadiya become a famous chef?
   a. by working in a restaurant
   b. by winning a TV baking competition
2. Where did she grow up?
   a. in the UK
   b. in Bangladesh
3. How does she feel about her nationality?
   a. very Bangladeshi
   b. very British
4. Why is Nadiya's family celebrating in the UK?
   a. She won a baking competition.
   b. She's traveling to Bangladesh.
5. What is one reason Nadiya wants to go to Bangladesh?
   a. to learn about the culture and food
   b. to learn about life in a big city
6. Why does Nadiya cry when she sees her family in Bangladesh?
   a. They aren't happy to see her.
   b. She realizes she missed them.

C. DISCUSS Ask and answer the questions with a partner.

1. In the video, we're told that Nadiya's grandmother is very important to her. Why do you think this is so?
2. What do you think Nadiya will learn from the rest of her travels in Bangladesh? How will the experience change her?

SAY WHAT YOU THINK

SYNTHESIZE Think about the unit video, Listening 1, and Listening 2 as you discuss the questions.

1. Many families in the world today have family members who live in different countries. How does this affect family life? What are the advantages and disadvantages?
2. How important is it to keep in touch with your larger family, that is aunts, uncles, cousins, grandparents, and so on?
3. Who has been an important person in your life? It might be a family member or other person. Why is the person important?

LISTENING 2   103

VOCABULARY SKILL Word families: verbs, nouns, adjectives

Word families are groups of words usually based on the same *root* or *headword*. When you learn a new word, try to learn different forms of the word at the same time. You can often find word families listed together in dictionaries.

verb	noun	adjective
inform	information	informative

iQ RESOURCES Go online to watch the Vocabulary Skill Video.
Resources > Video > Unit 3 > Vocabulary Skill Video

A. CATEGORIZE Complete the chart with other forms of the words. Use a dictionary to help you.

Verb	Noun	Adjective
participate	participant	participatory
coincide		
differ		
identify		
tend		

B. APPLY Complete each sentence with the correct word from Activity A. Use a dictionary to check your answers.

1. I can't __identify__ the person in this old photo. Is that my grandfather or his brother?

2. Everyone in my mother's family has a(n) _____ to be very thin. It's in their DNA, I guess.

3. My sister and I look very _____ from one another. I'm blond and blue-eyed, but she has dark hair and brown eyes.

4. Amy was a(n) _____ in the study group. She thought the experience was worth her time. She was glad to help.

5. I was on the bus the other day, and I ran into an old friend I haven't seen in years. What a(n) _____! I didn't know he lived near me.

iQ PRACTICE Go online for more practice with word families.
Practice > Unit 5 > Activity 10

SPEAKING

OBJECTIVE ▶ At the end of this unit, you are going to give a short speech about a quotation related to the idea of family. You will explain the quotation and then give your opinion about it. After listening to classmates' speeches, you will have a chance to ask questions.

GRAMMAR Auxiliary verbs in questions

Most questions in English are formed with an **auxiliary verb**, sometimes called a *helping verb*. This is true for all tenses. The basic pattern in questions is **auxiliary verb + subject + main verb**. This is true for *Yes/No questions* and for *information questions* that begin with question words. Study the examples in the charts. Note that in the *simple present* and *simple past* the main verb is always in base form.

yes/no questions

auxiliary verb	subject	main verb	(rest of sentence)
Did	the twins and their brother	have	a good relationship?
Is	Hal	searching	for his mother?
Do	you	agree	with Chris Rock?

information questions

question word	auxiliary verb	subject	main verb	(rest of sentence)
What	does	it	mean	to be part of a family?
How	can	you	explain	this?
Who	did	Faris	look like?	
Why	do	family members	help	each other?

SPEAKING **105**

A. COMPOSE Write *Yes/No* questions with the words.

1. they / study (present) / math at school

   Do they study math at school?

2. your grandfather / come (past) / here from Lebanon in the 1900s

   _____

3. Andrew / have (present) / a twin brother

   _____

4. he / want (present) / to go to Ireland next week

   _____

B. COMPOSE Write information questions with the words.

1. why / Henry Louis Gates / use (past) / DNA in the study

   Why did Henry Louis Gates use DNA in the study?

2. how / you / find out (past) / about your family history

   _____

3. who / your son / look like (present)

   _____

4. what / the twins / do (present continuous) / today

   _____

C. CREATE Work with a partner. Imagine that you are talking to Dr. Bashir in Listening 1 and the speaker in Listening 2. Write two questions you would like to ask each person.

Listening 1: "Twins in the Family"

1. _____
2. _____

Listening 2: "Family History"

1. _____
2. _____

D. DISCUSS Share your questions with another pair of students. Discuss possible answers.

iQ PRACTICE Go online for more practice with auxiliary verbs in questions.
Practice › Unit 5 › Activities 11–12

PRONUNCIATION Intonation in questions with *or*

Some questions offer the listener two choices. The choices are usually connected with the word *or*. These questions usually have rising-falling **intonation**. This is true for both *Yes/No* and information questions with *or*.

Are we just born that way or is it the influence of our families?

Is the man in the picture your brother or your cousin?

Does your twin brother like the same food as you or different food?

Are you more similar to your mother or your father?

 A. APPLY Listen to the questions. Then repeat them, using the same intonation that you hear.

1. Do you look more like your mother or your father?
2. Which do you think is more important: your DNA or your life experience?
3. Was the meeting a coincidence, or did they plan it?
4. Do you spend more time with your friends or your family?

B. EXTEND Work with a partner. Take turns asking the questions. Practice saying the questions with the correct intonation. Then write two more questions with *or*. Practice saying them.

1. Do you learn faster by reading a book or by listening to a teacher?
2. Which do you use more: a telephone or a computer?
3. Do you like to watch TV at night or read a book?
4. _____
5. _____

iQ PRACTICE Go online for more practice with intonation in questions with *or*.
Practice > Unit 5 > Activity 13

SPEAKING SKILL   Expressing opinions

When you express an **opinion**, you usually introduce your idea with words that signal an opinion. This is also true when you are explaining another person's opinion. Look at these examples:

> **In my view**, stories like this show that we are born with a tendency to have certain personality characteristics.
>
> **For me**, friends and family are different, even though I love both.
>
> **I feel that** I now understand more about myself and where I come from.
>
> **In the writer's opinion**, no one should have to have a DNA analysis.

Using phrases like these says to the listener, *"This is an opinion. It's not a fact. You don't have to agree."*

 A. IDENTIFY Listen to the speakers express opinions. Write the phrases they use to introduce their opinions.

1. _____
2. _____
3. _____
4. _____
5. _____

TIP FOR SUCCESS

Opinions are often the main ideas of a speech or presentation. Pay attention to special phrases that signal an opinion. They will help you find main ideas.

B. DISCUSS Work with a partner. Take turns answering the questions and expressing your opinions. Use expressions from the Speaking Skill box and other expressions you know to signal your opinions.

1. Which of these people is more a part of your family: a cousin you never met or your best friend? Why?

2. How do you define the word *home*?

3. "A gram of blood is worth more than a kilogram of friendship" is a Spanish proverb. What does this mean to you?

iQ PRACTICE   Go online for more practice with expressing opinions.
Practice > Unit 5 > Activity 14

108   UNIT 5   What does it mean to be part of a family?

UNIT ASSIGNMENT Give a short speech

OBJECTIVE ▶

In this section, you are going to give a short speech about families. As you prepare your speech, think about the Unit Question, "What does it mean to be part of a family?" Use information from Listening 1, Listening 2, the unit video, and your work in this unit to support your speech. Refer to the Self-Assessment checklist on page 110.

CONSIDER THE IDEAS

INVESTIGATE Read the quotations about families. Then discuss them in a group. What does each quotation mean?

> "A family is a unit composed not only of children, but of men, women . . . and the common cold."
> – Ogden Nash (poet and humorist, 1902–1971)

> "Family isn't about whose blood you have. It's about who you care about."
> – Trey Parker and Matt Stone (writers, 1998)

> "Happiness is having a large, loving, caring family—in another city."
> – George Burns (comedian and writer, 1896–1996)

> "A person sometimes needs to separate himself from family and friends and go to new places in order to change."
> – Katherine Butler Hathaway (writer, 1890–1942)

PREPARE AND SPEAK

A. GATHER IDEAS Choose one of the quotations above to create a short speech. Your speech should answer these questions.

1. What do you think the quotation means?
2. Do you agree or disagree with the quotation? Why?

B. ORGANIZE IDEAS Use the chart to make notes for your speech. Do not write complete sentences in the chart. Take only five minutes to do this.

Quotation	
Meaning of the quotation	
My opinion about the quotation	

C. SPEAK Work in a group. Give a short speech about the quotation you chose. Follow these rules for the speeches. Refer to the Self-Assessment checklist below before you begin.

1. Each person should speak for exactly two minutes—no more and no less.
2. One member of the group keeps track of the time for each speaker. Give the speaker a signal, such as a raised hand, after 1 minute 30 seconds. This means there are just 30 seconds left.
3. If the speaker stops before two minutes, someone in the group should ask a question to help him or her continue.
4. After two minutes, the speaker must stop talking.

D. DISCUSS Ask and answer these questions with your group.

1. How did you feel about giving your speech? Were you nervous or relaxed?
2. Was the speech easy or difficult for you? Why?
3. Did other members of the group understand your speech?

iQ PRACTICE Go online for your alternate Unit Assignment.
Practice > Unit 5 > Activity 15

CHECK AND REFLECT

A. CHECK Think about the Unit Assignment as you complete the Self-Assessment checklist.

SELF-ASSESSMENT	Yes	No
I was able to speak easily about the topic.	☐	☐
My group understood me.	☐	☐
I used auxiliary verbs in questions.	☐	☐
I used vocabulary from the unit.	☐	☐
I expressed my opinion.	☐	☐
I used intonation in questions with *or*.	☐	☐

B. REFLECT Discuss these questions with a partner or group.

1. What is something new you learned in this unit?
2. Look back at the Unit Question—What does it mean to be part of a family? Is your answer different now than when you started this unit? If yes, how is it different? Why?

iQ PRACTICE Go to the online discussion board to discuss the questions.
Practice > Unit 5 > Activity 16

TRACK YOUR SUCCESS

iQ PRACTICE Go online to check the words and phrases you have learned in this unit. *Practice › Unit 5 › Activity 17*

Check (✓) the skills you learned. If you need more work on a skill, refer to the page(s) in parentheses.

NOTE-TAKING	☐ I can use a simple outline to take notes. (p. 92)
LISTENING	☐ I can listen for reasons and explanations. (p. 97)
CRITICAL THINKING	☐ I can make judgments about the importance of information and ideas. (p. 102)
VOCABULARY	☐ I can use verbs, nouns, and adjectives from word families. (p. 104)
GRAMMAR	☐ I can use auxiliary verbs in questions. (p. 105)
PRONUNCIATION	☐ I can use intonation in questions with *or*. (p. 107)
SPEAKING	☐ I can express opinions. (p. 108)
OBJECTIVE ▸	☐ I can gather information and ideas to give a speech about families.

Behavioral Science

NOTE-TAKING	reviewing and editing notes
LISTENING	listening for dates and other numbers
CRITICAL THINKING	identifying "false" inferences
VOCABULARY	word families: suffixes
GRAMMAR	imperative verbs
PRONUNCIATION	word stress
SPEAKING	giving instructions

UNIT QUESTION

How can playing games be good for you?

A. Discuss these questions with your classmates.

1. "Playing games is a waste of time." Do you agree with this statement? Why or why not?
2. What games did you play as child? Do you ever play games now? If so, which ones?
3. Look at the photo. What kind of game are the women playing?

 B. Listen to *The Q Classroom* online. Then answer these questions.

1. What good things do Yuna and Marcus say about games like soccer and chess?
2. What does Felix say about how games can help us?
3. Why does Sophy think that games are a good social activity?

iQ PRACTICE Go to the online discussion board to discuss the Unit Question with your classmates. *Practice > Unit 6 > Activity 1*

UNIT OBJECTIVE

Listen to a talk and a news report. Gather information and ideas to develop and present an educational game.

NOTE-TAKING SKILL Reviewing and editing notes

It is important to review your notes as soon as possible after taking them. When you take notes, you write only single words and short phrases. If you wait too long, you might forget what these mean or why they are important. As you review your notes, edit them and add more information. Your notes will then be a more useful tool for studying. Note: It is a good idea to leave space on the page when you take notes, so you can add more information later.

 A. INVESTIGATE Listen to a short talk about the board game Monopoly. Then review one student's notes. Fill in the blanks and add other information you remember.

Monopoly

Lizzie Magie's Landlord

Monopoly
A. About game
   3rd most pop. game
   about buy and _____
   players pay rent when _____
   Goal = win _____
B. History
   Invent Charles Darrow 19____
   Darrow got idea earlier game: _____
   _____ Lizzie Magie 1903
   Different rules: _____ pay some rent to
   Public Treasury
   All players got share _____
C. Conclusion _____
_____

 B. ANALYZE Compare your notes with a partner. Listen again, if necessary.

iQ PRACTICE Go online for more practice with reviewing and editing notes.
Practice > Unit 6 > Activity 2

LISTENING SKILL Listening for dates and other numbers

Dates and other **numbers** are often important details when you are listening, whether a friend is telling a story or you're listening to a news report or a lecture.

Pay attention to numbers and dates as you listen. If possible, write them down with brief notes to remind yourself why they are important.

 A. APPLY Look at the dates and numbers in the box. Listen to the short talk about the word game Scrabble™. Then complete each sentence with the correct information.

| 1948 | 1938 | 1952 | 1991 | 4 | 25 | 100 |

1. Alfred Mosher Butts invented the game of Scrabble in _____.
2. In _____, Butts and his partner, James Brunot, started a Scrabble factory.
3. Between _____ and 2000, people bought more than _____ million Scrabble games.
4. One out of every _____ families in the United States has a Scrabble game in their home.
5. Scrabble is played in more than _____ languages around the world.
6. The first World Scrabble Championship was in _____.

Scrabble™

B. EXTEND Work with a partner. Practice listening for dates and numbers.

1. Write two original sentences about any topic, each one with a year and another number.

   Example: In 2017, there were 3,500 students in my university.

   a. _____
   b. _____

2. Read your sentences to a partner and listen to your partner's sentences. Say the dates and numbers you hear.

iQ PRACTICE Go online for more practice with listening for dates and other numbers. *Practice › Unit 6 › Activity 3*

LISTENING

LISTENING 1 **Why Should Adults Play Video Games?**

OBJECTIVE ▶ You are going to listen to a game developer give an informal talk about the benefits of video games for adults. As you listen, gather information and ideas about how playing games can be good for you.

VOCABULARY SKILL REVIEW

In Unit 5, you learned about word families. Look at the underlined words in Activity A. Can you find other word forms for them? Use a dictionary if needed.

PREVIEW THE LISTENING

A. VOCABULARY Here are some words from Listening 1. Read the sentences. Then choose the answer that best matches the meaning of each underlined word.

1. A game <u>developer</u> needs to have a lot of fresh, new ideas for games. He or she must be a good computer programmer.

    a. person who makes things

    b. person who sells things

2. Before deciding which sport to practice, you need to consider the <u>benefits</u> of each one.

    a. prices

    b. good points

3. These days, it is possible to have many forms of <u>entertainment</u>, such as games and music, in your own home.

    a. things that are fun and interesting

    b. things that help people work

4. That math program has had a <u>positive</u> effect on my son. He's beginning to understand algebra very well.

   a. good

   b. bad

5. The <u>object</u> of the game of Scrabble is to win the most points with the words you make.

   a. place

   b. goal

6. You've been under a lot of <u>stress</u> lately. Let's play a game! It'll help you feel better.

   a. state of worry

   b. state of being happy

7. Knowing how to speak in public is a <u>useful</u> skill. Sometimes you will have to make a presentation at work.

   a. not making a mistake

   b. helpful for doing something

8. You never know how someone will <u>react</u> when they lose a game.

   a. do or say something because of something else that happened

   b. tell a lot of people about something that happened

> **ACADEMIC LANGUAGE**
> The word *benefit* is often used in academic speaking and writing. It can be used to draw attention to a point to consider. *Consider the benefits of decreasing stress by the simple act of playing video games.*
>
> **OPAL**
> Oxford Phrasal Academic Lexicon

iQ PRACTICE Go online for more practice with the vocabulary.
Practice > Unit 6 > Activities 4–5

B. PREVIEW You are going to listen to a game developer talk about video games. Who do you think plays video games more, children or adults? Why?

LISTENING 1

WORK WITH THE LISTENING

TIP FOR SUCCESS
When listening to a talk or lecture, sit slightly forward in your seat. This position will help you concentrate, and you will understand more.

 A. IDENTIFY Listen to a talk about the benefits of playing video games. The speaker will mention four benefits. Number the pictures in the order you hear them.

Reduce stress

Improve hand-eye coordination

Use as a learning tool

Practice skills useful in the workplace

iQ RESOURCES Go online to download extra vocabulary support.
Resources > Extra Vocabulary > Unit 6

 B. LISTEN AND TAKE NOTES Prepare the chart for taking notes. Write the four benefits from Activity A. Then listen again and take notes on the examples the speaker uses to illustrate each benefit.

	Benefits	Examples
1		
2		
3		
4		

C. APPLY Listen again. Complete the sentences with the missing information.

1. In 2018, _____ percent of video gamers were over 18 years of age.

2. Of these, _____ percent were _____ years of age or older.

118 UNIT 6 How can playing games be good for you?

3. Surgeons who played video games at least _____ hours per week made _____ percent fewer mistakes.

4. More than _____ percent of students who played educational games felt that the games helped them understand subjects like history and math.

D. **CATEGORIZE** Read the statements. Write *T* (true) or *F* (false). Then work with a partner to correct the false statements.

___ 1. The speaker admits that there can be problems with playing video games too often.

___ 2. Games about historical events cannot be both entertaining and educational.

___ 3. The speaker says that skills used in video games are not useful at work.

___ 4. Playing fast-action games is very exciting but also creates stress.

___ 5. Video games can have positive effects on a player's feelings.

___ 6. The speaker thinks parents should play video games with their children.

E. **EXPLAIN** Work with a partner. Ask and answer the questions. Give examples and explanations as you discuss each question.

1. How do video games improve hand-eye coordination?
2. How can video games help students study subjects like math and history?
3. What features of video games may help users relax and reduce stress?

iQ PRACTICE Go online for additional listening and comprehension.
Practice > Unit 6 > Activity 6

SAY WHAT YOU THINK

DISCUSS Discuss the questions in a small group.

1. In the listening, the speaker reported that more adults play video games than children. Did this fact surprise you? Why or why not?

2. Do you think that playing video games is an appropriate activity for an adult? Why or why not?

3. The speaker mentions that video gamers may spend too much time playing games. What other problems might people have with playing video games?

LISTENING 2 Chess Champions

OBJECTIVE ▶ You are going to listen to a news report about children who play chess. As you listen, gather information and ideas about how playing games can be good for you.

PREVIEW THE LISTENING

A. VOCABULARY Here are some words from Listening 2. Read the definitions. Then complete each sentence with the correct word.

> **apply** *(verb)* OPAL to make practical use of something
> **coach** *(noun)* a person who trains people to compete in a sport or game
> **competitive** *(adjective)* eager to win or be more successful than others
> **disappointment** *(noun)* the state of being disappointed, sad because you did not succeed at something
> **lose** *(verb)* to not win; to be defeated in a game
> **pressure** *(noun)* OPAL an unhappy feeling caused by the need to succeed or to behave in a particular way
> **tournament** *(noun)* a competition in which many players or teams play against each other
> **wonderful** *(adjective)* very good; giving great pleasure

Oxford 3000™ words   **OPAL** Oxford Phrasal Academic Lexicon

1. That player is too _____. He wants to win every game and feels angry when he doesn't.
2. The _____ taught the team the rules of the game and helped them develop good strategies.
3. If the children _____ his ideas, they will be better players.
4. It's a big _____ when you don't win, but you can learn a lot from losing.
5. Our club is going to play in an important chess _____ next month. Teams from all over the city will be there.
6. Your team won all your games. Congratulations! That's _____!
7. In chess, even if you think that you do everything right, you can still _____ the game.
8. Parents shouldn't put a lot of _____ on their children by telling them they have to win every game.

iQ PRACTICE Go online for more practice with the vocabulary.
Practice > Unit 6 > Activities 7–8

B. PREVIEW You are going to listen to a news report about children who play chess. Work with a partner. Answer the questions.

1. What do you know about the game of chess? Discuss.

2. Work with your partner to identify the chess pieces in the pictures. Write the correct name under each picture.

---
king   queen   knight   bishop

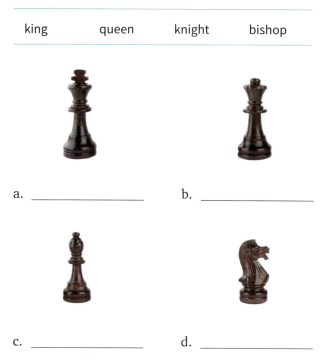

a. _____   b. _____

c. _____   d. _____

3. How can children benefit from playing a game like chess?

WORK WITH THE LISTENING

A. INVESTIGATE Listen to the news report. Don't take notes. Work with a partner to discuss what you each remember hearing.

B. LISTEN AND TAKE NOTES Listen to the news report again. Take notes using the headings in the chart.

Benefits of playing chess	
Does chess cause stress?	
What to do when children lose a game	

C. IDENTIFY Read the questions. Choose the correct answers. Use your notes to help you.

1. When do some schools now offer chess clubs and classes?
   a. only in high school
   b. starting in kindergarten
   c. starting in the fourth grade

2. Who did the Panda Pawns compete against in their chess tournament?
   a. college students
   b. elementary school students
   c. high school students

3. How did the young player named Lauren say that chess helped her?
   a. It helped her learn the different moves in the game.
   b. It helped her learn to think ahead in real-life situations.
   c. It helped her make new friends with other chess players.

4. What did the coach say he liked about chess?
   a. Players have to take time to think.
   b. It's a fast game and players have to think fast.
   c. Technology is making it a better game.

5. What did Dr. Ochoa think about the children's experience at the tournaments?

   a. They were excited and seemed to have a wonderful time.

   b. The competition put them under too much stress.

   c. Their teachers made them feel that winning was very important.

6. Which statement would Dr. Ochoa probably NOT agree with?

   a. Playing chess should be fun for children.

   b. Playing chess will help children later in their lives.

   c. Playing chess causes too much stress when a child loses.

CRITICAL THINKING STRATEGY

Identifying "false" inferences

An **inference** is a logical conclusion. It is an idea that you decide is probably true based on the information you have. It is reasonable and makes good sense. In this example, the information strongly supports the conclusion, or inference. Note that the inference is probable, or likely, but not certain.

Information	Inference
Jacob has just finished playing a chess game. He doesn't look very happy.	He probably lost the game.

Sometimes people make "false" inferences. In these cases, there is not enough information to support the conclusion.

Information	False inference
An eight-year-old boy from Nigeria won a New York State chess tournament.	People from Nigeria are great chess players.

The fact that one person, or even many people, from a country are good at something does not mean that everyone is.

iQ PRACTICE Go online to watch the Critical Thinking Video and check your comprehension. *Practice > Unit 6 > Activity 9*

D. ANALYZE Read the sentences. Check the correct box for each sentence: "Supported inference" or "False inference" based on the news report. Hint: There are two of each.

	Supported inference	False inference
1. Many schools believe that playing chess is good for their students.	☐	☐
2. Dr. Ochoa thinks all schools should have chess clubs like the Panda Pawns.	☐	☐
3. Many parents get angry when their child loses a game.	☐	☐
4. Losing a game can be a good learning experience.	☐	☐

E. EXPLAIN Compare answers with a partner. Explain why each answer is either a supported inference or a false one.

WORK WITH THE VIDEO

A. PREVIEW Do you think playing video games in school could help students learn? How?

VIDEO VOCABULARY

engage (v.) to interest or attract someone to something

assess (v.) to judge or form an opinion about something

impact (n.) an effect or impression made on someone or something

simulate (v.) to imitate the appearance or character of something

power plant (n.) a place where electricity is generated

zone (n.) an area with a particular use, for example, for homes or businesses

iQ RESOURCES Go online to watch the video about using video games in the classroom. *Resources > Video > Unit 6 > Unit Video*

B. CATEGORIZE Watch the video two or three times. Read the statements. Write *T* (true) or *F* (false).

_____ 1. Jessica Lindl, the narrator in the video, says that bringing video games into the classroom will help prepare students for success in the 21st century.

_____ 2. Lindl thinks the education system has already changed and is taking advantage of new technology.

_____ 3. She thinks that since playing video games has become so common, it's easier for people to imagine using games in the classroom.

_____ 4. In the video game called SimCity, students solve real-world problems in a simulated city.

_____ 5. Lindl says that moving from one level to another in a video game by learning certain skills is similar to taking tests to make progress in school.

_____ 6. In the example Lindl gives about SimCity, a city has a major problem with its water supply.

_____ 7. Many kids playing SimCity tried to solve the problem by turning off all the power plants. That was the correct decision.

_____ 8. Lindl thinks that most schools are preparing students for success by using new technology and innovations.

C. EXTEND Jessica Lindl believes that bringing video games into the classroom will help prepare students for life in the 21st century. Do you agree or disagree with this idea? Why?

SAY WHAT YOU THINK

SYNTHESIZE Think about the unit video, Listening 1, and Listening 2 as you discuss the questions.

1. Think about games or sports you play frequently. What can you learn from playing them? How can they make learning easier?

2. Listening 1 and Listening 2 mention games as a form of entertainment, as something "fun." How important is fun in our lives?

3. Do you agree with the following statement? Why or why not?

    "We don't stop playing because we grow old; we grow old because we stop playing."
    – George Bernard Shaw (playwright, 1856–1950)

VOCABULARY SKILL Word families: suffixes

A **suffix** is a word or syllable placed after a root word. A suffix often changes the part of speech of the word. For example, the suffixes *-ion* or *-tion* often mark the change from a verb to a noun. Adding the suffix sometimes results in other spelling changes. Here are some examples.

verb	noun
compete	compet**ition**
produce	prod**uction**
react	reac**tion**

A. APPLY Complete the chart with the noun form of each verb. Use the suffixes *-ion* or *-tion*. Use a dictionary to check for possible spelling changes.

Verb	Noun
coordinate	
discuss	
inform	
instruct	
operate	
pronounce	

B. APPLY Complete each sentence with the noun form of the verb in parentheses. Use a dictionary to check spelling if necessary.

1. The _____ (present) of the prizes will take place on the last day of the competition.

2. The teacher will make the _____ (introduce), and then the winners will speak.

3. Who made the _____ (decide) to start a chess club?

4. More than one person worked to develop the game. It was a _____ (create) based on the work of many departments.

5. Thomas Edison had little formal _____ (educate). His mother taught him at home.

iQ PRACTICE Go online for more practice with suffixes.
Practice > Unit 6 > Activity 10

128   UNIT 6   How can playing games be good for you?

SPEAKING

OBJECTIVE ▶ At the end of this unit, you are going to work in a group to develop an educational game. As part of the game development, you will have to give instructions to the players.

GRAMMAR Imperative verbs

Use affirmative and negative **imperatives** to give instructions and directions.

For affirmative imperatives, use **the base form of the verb**.

- **Raise** your hands.
- **Look** at the people around you.

For negative imperatives, use **do not** or **don't** + the base form of the verb. *Don't* is more common when speaking. Using *do not* when speaking can make the imperative sound stronger.

- **Don't spend** too much time playing games.
- **Do not move** your queen there!

In imperative sentences, *you* is "understood" as the subject of the verb. We don't usually say or write the word *you*. However, when you are giving a long list of instructions, using *you* from time to time sounds more polite.

- Next, **you** move the queen out to attack.

iQ RESOURCES Go online to watch the Grammar Skill Video.
Resources > Video > Unit 6 > Grammar Skill Video

A. APPLY Complete the conversation. Use the imperative phrases in the box. Then practice the conversation with a partner.

| do *not* tell | don't say | put up one finger |
| take one | use your hands | you act out |

Khalid: We're playing charades. Do you want to play?

Max: Charades? What's that? I've never heard of it.

Khalid: It's a game. You act out things, and the other players have to guess them. We're acting out common activities.

Max: Sounds interesting. I'd like to try it.

Khalid: Good. Just do as I say. First, _____ of the cards from this box and read it silently. _____ anyone what it says.

Max: OK. I did that. And now?

Khalid: Now, you are on our team. Next, _____ what it says. _____ and your body, but _____ anything. Then we try to guess what it is.

Max: You mean I can't talk at all?

Khalid: That's right. There are things you can do for some common words. For example, _____ for the number one, two for two, etc. Make a *T* with your fingers and it means the word *the*.

Max: OK. Here goes. I'll give it a try.

Khalid: You're driving a car!

Max: That's right. Hey, that was easy. Khalid, now it's your turn.

🔊 **B. EVALUATE** Listen and check your answers.

C. CREATE Work with a partner. Tell your partner how to do something. Use imperative verbs. Choose one of the topics below or use your own idea.

- How to send an email
- How to learn a new word
- How to remember people's names
- How to lose a game politely

iQ PRACTICE Go online for more practice with imperative verbs.
Practice > Unit 6 > Activity 11

iQ PRACTICE Go online for the Grammar Expansion: imperative sentences.
Practice > Unit 6 > Activity 12

PRONUNCIATION Word stress

When learning the pronunciation of a word, it is important to know which syllable to stress. If you put the stress on the wrong syllable, the listener might not understand it. The position of the stressed syllable varies in words with three or more syllables.

Notice where the main stress falls in these words.

1st syllable	2nd syllable	3rd syllable
be-ne-fit	im-**por**-tance	en-ter-**tain**-ment

There are some patterns that can help you decide which syllable to stress. For example, words ending with the suffix –*tion* stress the syllable before the suffix.

ed-u-**ca**-tion   com-pe-**ti**-tion

Sometimes you have to look up a word in the dictionary or ask someone to say the word for you to learn the correct pronunciation. When English speakers see a word they don't know, they often ask, "How do you pronounce this word?"

A. IDENTIFY Listen to the words. Underline the stressed syllable.

TIP FOR SUCCESS

Learning the correct pronunciation of a long word helps you remember the word. Then you will say it with the same stress and rhythm every time you use it.

Words with 3 syllables	Words with 4 syllables	Word with 5+ syllables
intro<u>duce</u>	competitive	elementary
excited	experience	coordination
messages	understanding	creativity

🔊 **B. APPLY** Listen to the words and repeat. Focus on using the correct stress.

1. positive
2. situation
3. wonderful
4. disappointment
5. organizers
6. tournament
7. developer
8. destruction

iQ PRACTICE Go online for more practice with word stress.
Practice > Unit 6 > Activity 13

SPEAKING SKILL Giving instructions

When you are giving **instructions** about how to do something, first give a general description of the task. For example, to tell someone how to play a game, give some general information about the game and tell them what the object of the game is. Then present the steps in the correct order. Use phrases like these to make your instructions clear.

> **The object of the game is to** score the most points.
> **Here's how to** act out the words in charades.

Use order words and phrases to make the sequence of the steps clear.

> **First**, take one of the cards from the box.
> **Next**, you have to act out what it says.
> **After that**, the other team takes a turn.
> **Finally**, the team with the most correct guesses wins the game.

🔊 **A. APPLY** Listen to the conversation about bowling. Complete the conversation with the words and phrases that make the instructions clear. Then practice the conversation with a partner.

Mi-rae: Is this your first time bowling? Don't worry. I can tell you how the game works.

Liana: OK. What do we do?

Mi-rae: Do you see those white things? They're called pins. The _____ of the game is to knock them down with a ball. You roll the
                    1
ball down the lane to hit them.

Bowling

Liana: That sounds easy. What do I do first?

Mi-rae: _____, choose a ball. Pick one that isn't too heavy
                2
for you.

Liana: OK. I think I'm going to use this ball. I really like the color. What do I do _____3_____ ?

Mi-rae: _____4_____ , you hold the ball with your fingers in the holes. _____5_____ , you stand in front of the lane. Do you understand so far?

Liana: Yes. I get it so far. _____6_____ what do I do? Do I roll it with both hands?

Mi-rae: No, the _____7_____ is to roll it with one hand. _____8_____ , try to roll it down the middle of the lane.

Liana: OK. Wow! I knocked down all the pins!

Mi-rae: Great! That's called a strike. You're going to be good at bowling!

> **TIP FOR SUCCESS**
> Stop from time to time and check that listeners understand your instructions. Ask a specific question or say something like, "Are you with me so far?"

B. IDENTIFY Read the instructions about how to play hide and seek. Put the instructions in the correct order. Write 1 to 5 next to the sentences.

___ Then, the other players hide while the seeker counts.

___ Finally, players try to return to the base. A player who is tagged, or touched, by the seeker loses.

___ Second, the seeker stands at the base, closes his or her eyes, and counts to 20.

_1_ First, choose one player in the group to seek, or look for, the other players.

___ Next, the seeker tries to find the hidden players.

iQ PRACTICE Go online for more practice with giving instructions.
Practice › Unit 6 › Activity 14

Hide and seek

UNIT ASSIGNMENT **Develop and present an idea for a new game**

OBJECTIVE ▶ In this section, you are going to work in a group to develop an educational game that can help people in their real lives. It can be any kind of game: a video game, a board game, etc. You will then present it to the class. As you prepare your game, think about the Unit Question, "How can playing games be good for you?" Use information from Listening 1, Listening 2, the unit video, and your work in this unit to support your presentation. Refer to the Self-Assessment checklist on page 136.

CONSIDER THE IDEAS

A. INVESTIGATE Read these tips about developing games.

Home   🔍   Sign in

Game Development – How to get started!

To develop a game, it's a good idea to work with two or three other people. A group creates more ideas, and you can test the game to see how it's working. Here are a few tips to help you get started.

- First, think of a theme (main topic) for your game. It's usually more interesting if it's about some real-life situation such as work, travel, or family life.
- Next, narrow the topic so that it is something that is easily understood by the game players.
- Decide what kind of game it will be—a video game, a traditional board game, or perhaps a game that doesn't need any equipment, like charades.
- Decide what the goal of the game is. How do players move? How does someone win the game? Is it a video game with a story?
- Write a short list of possible rules. How does the game start? What do players do during the game? Is there anything players cannot do?
- List objects people will need to play the game. If possible, make some drawings to show what the game will look like.
- Test the game. Make sure that it is easy to play. Have other people test it, too.

The most important thing is to make sure the game is fun and easy to learn. Players should be able to learn something as they play.

B. DISCUSS Work in a group. Answer the questions.

1. Why is it better to work with a group to develop a game?
2. What kind of themes do the tips on page 134 suggest?
3. What are some of the most important things to do when you develop a game?

PREPARE AND SPEAK

A. GATHER IDEAS Work in a group. Agree on a theme for your game and decide what type of game it will be. Use an idea from the list below or think of your own idea.

- a game that helps people learn English
- a game that helps students learn about a kind of math
- a game about visiting other countries

B. ORGANIZE IDEAS With your group, develop a plan for your game. Use the tips on page 134. Follow these steps.

1. Discuss and plan the game. Remember to keep the game very simple.
2. Create a list of rules and collect the materials you need.
3. Prepare drawings or other items that will help with your presentation.
4. Practice the presentation. Make sure that everyone in the group has a part. The presentation should include these points:
   - The name and object of the game
   - The steps followed to play the game
   - Any special rules players need to know
   - An explanation of how the game ends
   - What players can learn by playing the game

C. SPEAK Give your presentation to the class or to another group. Refer to the Self-Assessment checklist on page 136 before you begin.

iQ PRACTICE Go online for your alternate Unit Assignment.
Practice > Unit 6 > Activity 15

CHECK AND REFLECT

A. CHECK Think about the Unit Assignment as you complete the Self-Assessment checklist.

SELF-ASSESSMENT	Yes	No
I was able to speak easily about the topic.	☐	☐
The class or my group understood me.	☐	☐
I used imperative verbs.	☐	☐
I used vocabulary from the unit.	☐	☐
I gave instructions.	☐	☐
I used correct word stress.	☐	☐

B. REFLECT Discuss these questions with a partner or group.

1. What is something new you learned in this unit?
2. Look back at the Unit Question—How can playing games be good for you? Is your answer different now than when you started the unit? If yes, how is it different? Why?

iQ PRACTICE Go to the online discussion board to discuss the questions.
Practice > Unit 6 > Activity 16

TRACK YOUR SUCCESS

iQ PRACTICE Go online to check the words and phrases you have learned in this unit. *Practice > Unit 6 > Activity 17*

Check (✓) the skills and strategies you learned. If you need more work on a skill, refer to the page(s) in parentheses.

NOTE-TAKING	☐ I can review and edit my notes. (p. 114)
LISTENING	☐ I can recognize dates and other numbers. (p. 115)
CRITICAL THINKING	☐ I can identify "false" inferences. (p. 124)
VOCABULARY	☐ I can recognize suffixes in word families. (p. 127)
GRAMMAR	☐ I can recognize and use imperative verbs. (p. 129)
PRONUNCIATION	☐ I can use correct word stress. (p. 131)
SPEAKING	☐ I can give clear instructions. (p. 132)
OBJECTIVE ▶	☐ I can gather information and ideas to develop and present an educational game.

Environmental Science

NOTE-TAKING	preparing to take notes in class
CRITICAL THINKING	categorizing
LISTENING	recognizing a speaker's attitude
VOCABULARY	compound nouns
GRAMMAR	future with *will*
PRONUNCIATION	word stress in compound nouns
SPEAKING	summarizing

UNIT QUESTION

How do people survive in extreme environments?

A. Discuss these questions with your classmates.

1. What do you think the term *extreme environment* means? Give examples.
2. Do you think you could survive in one of these extreme environments? Why or why not?
3. Look at the picture. Do you think many people live here? Why or why not?

🔊 **B.** Listen to *The Q Classroom* online. Then answer these questions.

1. What examples does Yuna give of extreme environments?
2. What example does Felix give?
3. How does Sophy explain Felix's example?
4. What possible extreme environment does Marcus talk about?

iQ PRACTICE Go to the online discussion board to discuss the Unit Question with your classmates. *Practice › Unit 7 › Activity 1*

UNIT OBJECTIVE ▶ Watch a video and listen to a follow-up discussion. Then listen to a news report. Gather information and ideas to role-play an interview about surviving in an extreme environment.

NOTE-TAKING SKILL Preparing to take notes in class

Before you go to a class, make sure you read all the assignments. They will often contain key words and ideas that the instructor will use in the classroom. As you read, write down these key words and ideas. Look up unfamiliar words to check their meaning and pronunciation. Pronunciation is important because it is sometimes difficult to recognize a word when you hear it in context, even if you know the word.

Use your "pre-class" notes in the classroom. Listen for the key words and add more information to your notes.

VOCABULARY SKILL REVIEW

In Unit 6, you learned about two common English suffixes that change a verb to a noun. Notice here that the suffix *-ic* changes the noun *nomad* to the adjective *nomadic*. What other suffixes can you identify in this introduction?

A. IDENTIFY Read the introduction to a video titled *The Nomads of Outer Mongolia* about a nomadic people known as the Darhad. Prepare notes and look up words you don't know in a dictionary. Check both meaning and pronunciation.

Outer Mongolia. Just hearing this name brings to mind a place that is far, far away. Mongolia is indeed a very remote country. It lies between China to the south and the Russian province of Siberia to the north. It is a landlocked country, which means that it is completely surrounded by land and has no coastline. It is also a country of extremes. Temperatures can fall to –40 degrees Celsius in the winter in the north and be as high as 40 degrees Celsius in the Gobi Desert in the southern part of the country.

Mongolia is a large country geographically—nineteenth in the world—with a small population of just over three million people. Because very little of the country is suitable for agriculture, raising animals is an important part of the economy. People raise sheep and cattle, as well as goats, horses, and camels. About 30 percent of the population, including the Darhad, still lead a traditional nomadic lifestyle. This means that during the year they move from place to place as they look for good pasture for their animals. They live in round, tent-like structures called *gers* or *yurts* that they can take down and carry with them from place to place.

Sheep and goats in a pasture

B. EXPLAIN What words did you look up? Compare with a partner.

iQ PRACTICE Go online for more practice with preparing to take notes in class. *Practice > Unit 7 > Activity 2*

140 UNIT 7 How do people survive in extreme environments?

LISTENING

LISTENING 1 The Nomads of Outer Mongolia

OBJECTIVE ▶ You are going to watch a video about the Darhad people. Then you will listen to a class discussion about it. As you watch and listen, gather information and ideas about how people survive in extreme environments.

A Mongolian yurt, or *ger*

PREVIEW THE LISTENING

ACADEMIC LANGUAGE
The word *attack* is common in academic speaking. It can be either a verb or a noun. *The wolf attacked the man, but luckily the man survived the attack.*

─────────── **OPAL**
Oxford Phrasal Academic Lexicon

A. VOCABULARY Here are some words from Listening 1. Read the definitions. Then complete each sentence with the correct word.

attack *(verb)* 🔑 OPAL to try to hurt or defeat someone by using force
fascinating *(adjective)* 🔑 extremely interesting
freezing *(adjective)* 🔑 very cold; the temperature at which water becomes ice, or freezes
permanent *(adjective)* 🔑 lasting a long time or forever; that will not change
process *(verb)* 🔑 OPAL to treat something (for example, with chemicals) in order to change it
remain *(verb)* 🔑 to be left after other people or things have gone
suitable *(adjective)* 🔑 OPAL right or convenient for someone or something
threat *(noun)* 🔑 OPAL a person or thing that may damage something or hurt someone

🔑 Oxford 3000™ words   **OPAL** Oxford Phrasal Academic Lexicon

LISTENING 1 **141**

1. There are a lot of trees around our house. When the weather is very dry, fire is a serious _____.

2. I'm going to a formal dinner. Is this green jacket _____? Maybe I should wear the black one and wear a tie.

3. We've lived here for 20 years, and we're not planning to move. It's our _____ home.

4. They will _____ in Florida until the winter is over and then come home.

5. We're expecting _____ weather tonight. I'm sure there will be ice on the lake in the morning!

6. If you think a wolf is going to _____ you, don't run. Shout and make yourself look scary.

7. We've just seen a _____ program about the Inuit people of northern Alaska. What an interesting way of life!

8. Over there, the workers _____ the cream and milk in order to make butter and ice cream.

iQ PRACTICE Go online for more practice with the vocabulary.
Practice > Unit 7 > Activities 3–4

B. **PREVIEW** You are going to watch the video *The Nomads of Outer Mongolia* and listen to a class discussion about it. What do you think is extreme about the environment in which the Darhad people live? Discuss this question with a partner. Give examples.

WORK WITH THE LISTENING

iQ RESOURCES Go online to watch the video.
Resources > Video > Unit 7 > Listening 1 Part 1

TIP FOR SUCCESS

When possible, watch movies or videos with English captions. This will improve your listening skills as you hear the words and read them at the same time. It is an enjoyable way to practice listening.

A. **LISTEN AND TAKE NOTES** Review your "pre-class" notes from Activity A on page 140. Then takes notes as you watch the video* and listen to the discussion.

iQ RESOURCES Go online to download extra vocabulary support.
Resources > Extra Vocabulary > Unit 7

*Audio version available. *Resources > Audio > Unit 7*

UNIT 7 How do people survive in extreme environments?

B. ANALYZE How did the Note-taking activity help you when you were taking notes?

C. IDENTIFY Read the sentences. Choose the answer that best completes each statement. Use your notes to help you.

1. Nomads are people who ____.
    a. live in one place all their lives
    b. travel from one place to another during the year
    c. make almost everything they need themselves
2. The Darhad people use their animals mostly ____.
    a. for food and clothing
    b. as protection from wolves
    c. to help them move around
3. The Darhad live in ____.
    a. small houses
    b. wooden buildings
    c. felt-lined tents
4. One danger the Darhad face is ____.
    a. traveling over the mountains
    b. herding their animals
    c. being attacked by wolves
5. The Darhad people move from place to place because ____.
    a. their animals need good places to find food
    b. it isn't safe for them to stay in one place
    c. they need to buy things from traders
6. The Darhad ____ in order to buy things from traders.
    a. have to use cash
    b. can use things they make such as cheese
    c. have to travel to the city
7. Felt is a material that the Darhad use ____.
    a. to make their tents
    b. as a food for their animals
    c. when they buy things from traders

D. **EXPLAIN** Match each statement with a supporting idea given by one of the speakers. Listen to the discussion again to check your answers.

____ 1. Traders are also nomads in some ways.

____ 2. The Darhad's lifestyle seems like a healthy one.

____ 3. It's important for the Darhad to keep their traditional lifestyle.

____ 4. Many nomads are leaving and going to the cities.

____ 5. The nomadic life is very hard.

____ 6. The students would not be able to live like the Darhad people.

a. They think they will have a better life there.

b. They live close to nature and in a close community.

c. They travel around and sell things to the nomads.

d. They shouldn't let modern society change their customs.

e. The Darhad people know how to survive in an extreme environment.

f. They climb mountains in the winter when it is minus 40 degrees.

CRITICAL THINKING STRATEGY

Categorizing

When we **categorize** information, we separate items into groups according to certain criteria or characteristics. When categorizing, first decide what these criteria or characteristics will be. For example, a collection of books can be grouped by topic: fiction, history, science, etc. Or you could group them by author, or even by the colors of the covers for a decorative effect. It all depends on your reasons for categorizing.

iQ PRACTICE Go online to watch the Critical Thinking Video and check your comprehension. *Practice > Unit 7 > Activity 5*

E. **CATEGORIZE** The words in the list represent important parts of the Darhad people's lives. Write each word in the appropriate category in the chart.

camels	cheese	freezing	goats	milk
mountains	pastures	sheep	snow	tents
valleys	winter	wolves	yogurt	

Animals	Features of the land	Weather	Food and supplies

F. EXPLAIN Work with a partner. Say why each of the items in Activity F is important to the Darhad people.

iQ PRACTICE Go online for additional listening and comprehension.
Practice > Unit 7 > Activity 6

SAY WHAT YOU THINK

DISCUSS Discuss the questions in a small group.

1. What do you think is the most interesting thing about the Darhad way of life? Why?

2. Do you think you could survive life with the Darhad community? Why or why not?

3. Ellen thinks it is important for people like the Darhad to keep their traditional lifestyle. Jon thinks this is not realistic because many nomads are leaving to go live in the cities. Who do you agree with more, Ellen or Jon? Why?

LISTENING SKILL Recognizing a speaker's attitude

Speakers communicate **attitudes** and feelings through tone of voice as well as the words they use. The tone of voice can tell the listener if the speaker is serious or joking. It shows the speaker's feelings about the subject of a conversation—positive or negative.

If you can see the speaker, his or her body language and facial expressions can tell you a lot about the speaker's attitude. If you can't see the speaker, you have to guess the speaker's attitude from the tone of his or her voice.

🔊 **A. ANALYZE** Listen to part of the conversation again. What does each speaker's voice tell you about his or her attitude or feelings? Discuss the questions.

1. How does Ellen sound when Norah says she would like to live like the Darhad? That is, does Ellen sound angry, surprised, or confused?
2. How do you think Norah feels at first about Ellen's response? For example, is she happy, angry, or sad?

🔊 **B. INTERPRET** Listen to another conversation between Norah, Jon, and Ellen. Work with a partner. Ask and answer the questions.

TIP FOR SUCCESS

Different cultures and languages express attitudes and emotions differently when speaking. It takes time and experience to listen for and understand people's feelings.

1. How does Ellen sound when she first learns that Norah is going to Mongolia—surprised or angry?
2. What does Ellen say to Norah?
3. How does Norah feel about what Ellen says—surprised or angry?
4. Do you think Ellen was rude? Why or why not?
5. How do Ellen and Norah feel at the end of the conversation? Are they angry or happy? How do you know?

iQ PRACTICE Go online for more practice recognizing a speaker's attitude.
Practice > Unit 7 > Activity 7

146 UNIT 7 How do people survive in extreme environments?

LISTENING 2 High-Rise Living

OBJECTIVE ▶ You are going to listen to a news report about people's experiences living in high-rise buildings. As you listen, gather information and ideas about how people survive in extreme environments.

PREVIEW THE LISTENING

A. VOCABULARY Here are some words from Listening 2. Read the sentences. Then write each underlined word next to the correct definition.

1. At the meeting, each resident who lives in the building will have to vote for or against changing the paint colors.

2. Mount Everest is 8,848 meters high. At that height, there isn't enough air for people to breathe easily.

3. I live on the 40th floor of my building. I'm sometimes late for work because I have to wait for the elevator to get down to the first floor.

4. They live in a suburb of Boston, in an area about 30 minutes outside the city.

5. In 1964, the state of Alaska had an earthquake that measured 9.2. Many buildings were destroyed.

6. This is a great neighborhood. There are a lot of good stores and restaurants nearby.

7. They're waiting for Dave's response to the email. They need his answer before they make a decision.

8. I felt the building shake just now. I think that big truck that drove by made it move.

a. _____ (verb) to move from side to side or up and down with short, quick movements

b. _____ (noun) a particular part of a city or town and the people who live there

c. _____ (noun) a person who lives in a place

d. _____ (noun) an answer or reaction to something

e. _____ (noun) the measurement from the bottom to the top of a person or thing

f. _____ (noun) a sudden, violent movement of the earth's surface

g. _____ (noun) a machine in a building that is used to carry people or things from one floor to another

h. _____ (noun) an area where people live that is outside the central city

iQ PRACTICE Go online for more practice with the vocabulary.
Practice > Unit 7 > Activities 8–9

B. PREVIEW You are going to listen to a news report about people who live in high-rise buildings. What do you think they will say about their experience? Name one thing.

WORK WITH THE LISTENING

 A. LISTEN AND TAKE NOTES Listen to the news report in which four people describe their experiences living in high-rise buildings. Are they mostly positive, negative, or both? On a sheet of paper, prepare a chart like the one below. As you listen, write the name of the city and mark each one as + (positive), – (negative), or *B* (both).

Person	City	Positive or negative	Notes
1.			
2.			
3.			
4.			

UNIT 7 How do people survive in extreme environments?

🔊 **B. EXPLAIN** Listen again and add information in your Notes column to explain how each person felt about living in a high-rise building.

C. EVALUATE Compare notes with a partner. Add to and edit your notes as needed.

D. EXPLAIN Answer the questions.

1. Why did the man from Singapore have a problem sleeping when he lived in a high-rise building?

2. How did he feel on windy days?

3. What are two things the woman in Toronto can see from her windows?

4. Is her apartment peaceful or noisy? Why?

5. Why did the family in London decide that the high-rise was not suitable for their family? Give one reason.

6. What did they do?

7. How does the woman in San Francisco feel about living in a high-rise building? Why?

8. What does she worry about?

E. CREATE Work in a small group. Follow these instructions.

1. Choose one topic from the list below. If possible, each person should choose a different topic.

   - High-rise living for families with children
   - Advantages of living in a high-rise building
   - Problems with living in a high-rise building
   - Are high-rise buildings safe, yes or no?

2. Tell the group everything you can about your topic. Use your notes to help you. You can also include your own ideas.

SAY WHAT YOU THINK

SYNTHESIZE Think about Listening 1 and Listening 2 as you discuss the questions.

1. Which lifestyle was more interesting for you to learn about, the nomadic life of the Darhad or life on a high floor in a high-rise building? Explain.
2. Have you ever lived in a high-rise building? If so, describe your experience. If not, would you like to? Why or why not?
3. What other extreme environments do people live in? What do you know about them?

VOCABULARY SKILL Compound nouns

A **compound noun** is a noun made up of two nouns or a noun and an adjective.

Some compound nouns are written as one word, like *coastline* (*coast* + *line*).

Others are written as two words, like *motion sickness*.

In a compound noun, the first word says something about the second word. A *coastline* is the outline that marks the coast of an area, or the border between the land and the sea. *Motion sickness* is the sick feeling caused by motion, often in a car, boat, or airplane.

A. APPLY Read the sentences. Then complete each compound noun with a word from the box. Use your dictionary to see if the compound noun is written as one word or two words.

TIP FOR SUCCESS
Check your dictionary to learn if a compound noun is written as one or two words.

| board | games | house | market |
| papers | quake | scrapers | style |

1. The strongest earth_____ ever recorded occurred in Chile in 1960. It measured 9.5.

2. Last year, we moved from a big city to a small town in the country. We have a very different life_____.

3. Each pet rock came in a card_____ box that looked like a box for carrying a pet.

4. Can you buy organic foods at that super_____?

5. Sometimes people refer to high-rise buildings as sky_____ because it looks as if they are touching the sky.

6. We have a little store_____ where we put things we don't need very often.

7. People still talk about news_____ even though they are reading them online, with no real "paper."

8. Many adults enjoy playing video_____ as much as or more than children do!

B. RESTATE Try to guess the compound nouns for these definitions. Some hints use both words of the compound word. Others don't.

1. A phone that is intelligent: _____a smartphone_____

2. A game in which players throw a ball through a net called a *basket*: _____

3. The light that comes from the sun: _____

4. Saturday and Sunday, two days at the end of the week: _____

5. A store where people can buy books: _____

6. What you call your mother's or father's mother: _____

iQ PRACTICE Go online for more practice with compound nouns.
Practice > Unit 7 > Activity 10

SPEAKING

OBJECTIVE ▶ At the end of this unit, you are going to work with a partner to role-play an interview about living in an extreme environment. As part of this role-play, you may have to summarize your or your partner's ideas.

GRAMMAR Future with *will*

Use **will + verb** to talk about the future, that is, about things that have not happened yet. Note that the form *will* never changes. It is the same for all persons and in singular and plural.

- One day people **will live** on Mars.
- She **will leave** next week.

Affirmative contraction

I will = I'll, they will = they'll, he will or *she will = he'll / she'll*

- **They'll allow** more people to live in a smaller area.

Negative contraction

will not = won't

- Humans **won't be** able to breathe the air on Mars.

Yes/No questions and short answers

will + subject + verb

- **Will you buy** an apartment in that building?
- Yes, I will. / No, I won't.

Information questions

Question word + *will* + subject + verb

- What **will Norah do** when she's with the Darhad people?

iQ RESOURCES Go online to watch the Grammar Skill Video.
Resources > Video > Unit 7 > Grammar Skill Video

A. APPLY Write sentences with *will* or *won't*. Use your own opinions.

1. Humans / travel / to Mars by 2030

   _____

2. Cities / build / more skyscrapers

   _____

3. The Darhad / continue / to live their traditional lifestyle

   _____

4. I probably / visit / Antarctica one day

   _____

5. Nomads / have / a better life in cities

   _____

6. Most people / be happier / in a high-rise building

   _____

B. EXPLAIN Work with a partner. Take turns answering and asking the questions with short answers. Use your own ideas.

A: Will you look for more information about the Darhad people?
B: Yes, I will. I'd like to learn more about them.

1. Will you ever travel to Antarctica?
2. Will you rent an apartment in a high-rise building?
3. Will you get motion-sick if you travel by boat?
4. Will you ever live in a place with an extreme environment?
5. Will you ever go mountain climbing?

iQ PRACTICE Go online for more practice with the future with *will*.
Practice > Unit 7 > Activity 11

iQ PRACTICE Go online for the Grammar Expansion: *be going to* and *will*.
Practice > Unit 7 > Activity 12

PRONUNCIATION Word stress in compound nouns

Compound nouns are pronounced as if they were one word. The **stress** is usually on the first syllable or word.

| <u>coast</u>line | <u>earth</u>quake | <u>life</u>style |
| <u>sky</u>scraper | <u>smart</u>phone | <u>store</u>house |

A. APPLY Listen and practice the pronunciation of these compound nouns.

1. bookstore
2. website
3. coffee cup
4. shoreline
5. newspaper
6. sunlight

A coastline

B. APPLY Work with a partner. Take turns reading these sentences aloud. Focus on the pronunciation of the compound nouns.

1. Mexico has coastlines along the Pacific Ocean and the Gulf of Mexico.
2. We went for a walk in the moonlight.
3. Those new lightbulbs are supposed to last for ten years.
4. Which sport do you prefer to play, basketball or football?
5. I prefer the lifestyle in the city. The country is too quiet for me.

iQ PRACTICE Go online for more practice with word stress in compound nouns. *Practice > Unit 7 > Activity 13*

SPEAKING SKILL Summarizing

To **summarize** means to present the main ideas of something you hear or read, but in a much shorter form, called a *summary*. A good summary:

- is short and clear.
- focuses on the main ideas, not the details.
- gives the speaker's ideas, not your opinions.

When speaking, you can summarize to:

- check your understanding of the main points in a conversation.
- tell someone briefly about something you heard or read.

A. EVALUATE Read the summaries of the video from Listening 1. Check (✓) the best summary. Why is it the best summary? Discuss with a partner.

The Nomads of Outer Mongolia

☐ 1. The video was about a group of nomads who live in Mongolia. They live in tents and have animals. Sometimes they buy things from traders. I don't think I'd like living the way the Darhad people do. For one thing, I really don't like cold weather or climbing mountains.

☐ 2. The video was about the lifestyle of the Darhad people, nomads in Mongolia. They travel from one place to another each year to find food for their animals. Their lives are difficult and full of danger such as attacks by wolves and extremely cold winters.

☐ 3. The video was about the Darhad people, who are nomads. They make most things they need themselves. They make cheese from milk from their animals. Sometimes they buy things from traders. It's very cold where they live.

B. RESTATE Work with a partner. Follow these instructions.

🔊 1. Listen to the news report.

Student A: Summarize the main ideas of the report.

Student B: Tell your partner if you agree with his or her summary.

🔊 2. Listen to the interview.

Student B: Summarize the main ideas of the interview.

Student A: Tell your partner if you agree with his or her summary.

iQ PRACTICE Go online for more practice with summarizing.
Practice > Unit 7 > Activity 14

UNIT ASSIGNMENT Role-play an interview

OBJECTIVE ▶ In this section, you are going to role-play an interview. As you prepare your role play, think about the Unit Question, "How do people survive in extreme environments?" Use information from Listening 1, Listening 2, and your work in this unit to prepare your role play. Refer to the Self-Assessment checklist on page 158.

CONSIDER THE IDEAS

A. **INVESTIGATE** Listen to the interview about an extreme environment. Number the interviewer's questions in the order you hear them, from 1 to 5.

____ How cold does it get in the winter?

____ Is it true that it's dark all the time in the winter?

____ What about food? What did you eat?

____ Have you ever lived in a really extreme environment?

____ How do you keep warm?

B. **INVESTIGATE** Listen again and take notes about Farouk's answers.

C. **CREATE** Work with a partner. Use the questions and your notes to act out the conversation. Answer the questions using your own words. Take turns being the interviewer.

PREPARE AND SPEAK

A. GATHER IDEAS Work with your partner. Prepare to role-play an interview.

1. Decide who will be the interviewer and who will be the person interviewed. Choose a topic for your interview. The topics below are just ideas to help you get started. You can use one of these or your own idea.

   - Living through a heat wave
   - Life in a very cold place
   - Life high in the mountains
   - Living in the desert
   - Living where it's very wet
   - Living on another planet

2. Make notes about all you know about your topic.

B. ORGANIZE IDEAS With your partner, plan the interview.

1. Make a list of questions for the interview.
2. Make notes for the answers to each one. (Don't write out the whole interview. Just make notes.)
3. Prepare a summary of the interview. The interviewer will end the interview with this summary.

C. SPEAK Practice your interview. Use intonation to express feelings during the interview. Present your interview to the class. Refer to the Self-Assessment checklist on page 158 before you begin.

iQ PRACTICE Go online for your alternate Unit Assignment.
Practice > Unit 7 > Activity 15

CHECK AND REFLECT

A. CHECK Think about the Unit Assignment as you complete the Self-Assessment checklist.

SELF-ASSESSMENT	Yes	No
I was able to speak easily about the topic.	☐	☐
My partner and the class understood me.	☐	☐
I used the future tense with *will*.	☐	☐
I used vocabulary from the unit.	☐	☐
I summarized the main ideas in the interview.	☐	☐
I used the correct word stress in compound nouns.	☐	☐

B. REFLECT Discuss these questions with a partner or group.

1. What is something new you learned in this unit?
2. Look back at the Unit Question—How do people survive in extreme environments? Is your answer different now than when you started this unit? If yes, how is it different? Why?

iQ PRACTICE Go to the online discussion board to discuss the questions.
Practice > Unit 7 > Activity 16

158 UNIT 7 How do people survive in extreme environments?

TRACK YOUR SUCCESS

iQ PRACTICE Go online to check the words and phrases you have learned in this unit. *Practice > Unit 7 > Activity 17*

Check (✓) the skills and strategies you learned. If you need more work on a skill, refer to the page(s) in parentheses.

NOTE-TAKING ☐ I can prepare to take notes in class. (p. 140)
CRITICAL THINKING ☐ I can categorize information. (p. 144)
LISTENING ☐ I can recognize a speaker's attitude. (p. 145)
VOCABULARY ☐ I can recognize and use compound nouns. (p. 150)
GRAMMAR ☐ I can recognize and use *will* to talk about the future. (p. 152)
PRONUNCIATION ☐ I can use correct word stress in compound nouns. (p. 153)
SPEAKING ☐ I can summarize information. (p. 154)

OBJECTIVE ▶ ☐ I can gather information and ideas to role-play an interview about surviving in extreme environments.

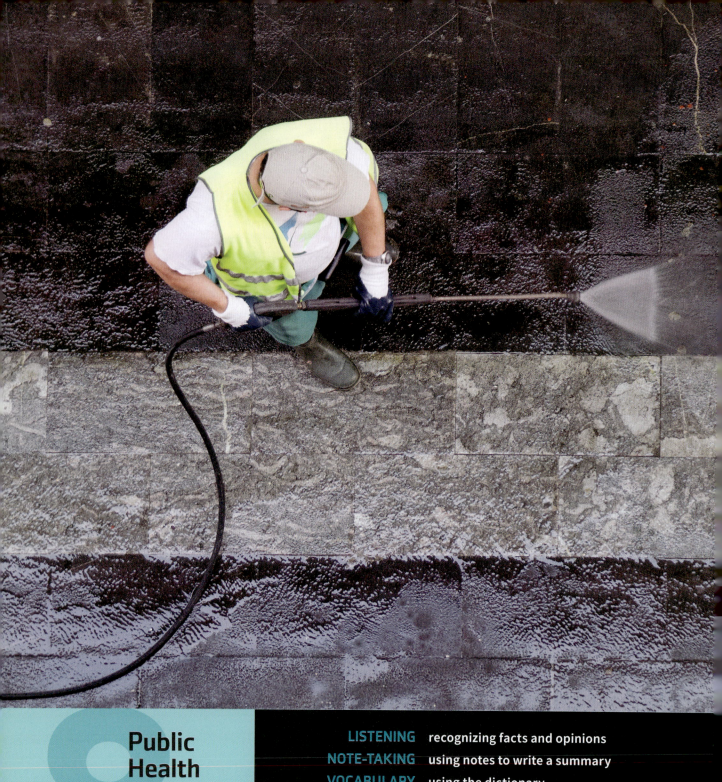

8 Public Health

LISTENING	recognizing facts and opinions
NOTE-TAKING	using notes to write a summary
VOCABULARY	using the dictionary
GRAMMAR	*if* clauses for future possibility
PRONUNCIATION	function words and stress
CRITICAL THINKING	appraising solutions to problems
SPEAKING	participating in a group discussion

 UNIT QUESTION

How important is cleanliness?

A. Discuss these questions with your classmates

1. Do you think you use a lot of water every day? Explain.
2. What did your parents tell you about cleanliness?
3. Look at the photo. What is the man doing? Do you think this is important?

🔊 **B.** Listen to *The Q Classroom* online. Then answer these questions.

1. How are Yuna's and Felix's answers to the question different?
2. What does Marcus say about the importance of clean water?
3. What does Sophy say about the other opinions?

iQ PRACTICE Go to the online discussion board to discuss the Unit Question with your classmates. *Practice › Unit 8 › Activity 1*

UNIT OBJECTIVE ▶ Watch a video and listen to a follow-up discussion. Then listen to a lecture. Gather information and ideas to participate in a discussion about the importance of clean water.

LISTENING

LISTENING 1 Water for Life

OBJECTIVE ▶

You are going to watch a video and then listen to a follow-up discussion about the importance of clean water. As you watch and listen, gather information and ideas about the importance of cleanliness.

PREVIEW THE LISTENING

A. VOCABULARY Here are some words and phrases from Listening 1. Choose the answer that has the meaning closest to the underlined word or phrase.

1. There is a <u>shortage</u> of fruit this year. The winter was too cold and many of the fruit trees died.

   a. large amount   b. not enough   c. too much

2. As the number of people increases, the <u>demand</u> for water also increases.

   a. need   b. kind   c. place

3. The <u>climate</u> here is good for crops. It rains often and it's not too cold.

   a. weather   b. land   c. ocean

4. The town tried to <u>prevent</u> the state from building another road. They didn't succeed, and the new roadwork begins this month.

   a. let   b. stop   c. allow

5. The tomato plants in my garden had a <u>disease</u>. Many of the leaves turned brown, and some of the plants died.

   a. energy   b. sickness   c. health

6. <u>Agriculture</u> uses a lot of water. Both animals and plants need water to be healthy.

   a. farming   b. city life   c. space

ACADEMIC LANGUAGE

The verb *prevent* is often used in academic English. It is sometimes used with the preposition *from* and an *-ing* verb. *The doctors prevented the disease from spreading.*

OPAL
Oxford Phrasal Academic Lexicon

7. Because there is a <u>lack of</u> water, we have to try to use less every day.

   a. not enough   b. too much   c. a lot of

8. Building another dam will have serious <u>consequences</u>. For example, some people who live near the river above the dam will lose their homes.

   a. ideas   b. problems   c. results

9. We need to have a good <u>supply</u> of food and water, in case of a storm. We'll need enough for two weeks.

   a. quality   b. type   c. amount

10. If more businesses come to the city, the population will <u>grow</u>.

    a. become smaller   b. get larger   c. decline

iQ PRACTICE Go online for more practice with the vocabulary.
Practice > Unit 8 > Activities 2–3

TIP FOR SUCCESS

Many students are nervous about listening. Relax! If you are nervous or stressed, it's more difficult to listen and understand what you hear.

B. PREVIEW You are going to watch a video and then listen to a group discussion about the importance of clean water. What are two problems you think the video or the discussion will mention? Discuss with a partner.

WORK WITH THE LISTENING

iQ RESOURCES Go online to watch the video.
Resources > Video > Unit 8 > Listening Part 1

A. LISTEN AND TAKE NOTES Create an outline like the one below. Watch the video* and then listen to the discussion. As you watch and listen, add ideas to your outline. Try to add a few key words in each section.

VOCABULARY SKILL REVIEW

In Unit 7, you learned about compound nouns. What compound nouns can you identify in Listening 1 Part 1?

iQ RESOURCES Go online to download extra vocabulary support.
Resources > Extra Vocabulary > Unit 8

Part 1: Video	Part 2: Discussion
A. Uses for water	A. Children and water-related disease
B. Things that take a lot of water to make	B. Population growth in cities
C. Sources of clean water	C. Water quality

*Audio version available. *Resources > Audio > Unit 8*

🔊 **B. EXPAND** Watch the video and listen to the discussion again. Add more information to your notes.

🔊 **C. IDENTIFY** Read the questions. Choose the correct answers. Use your notes to help you. Then watch and listen to check your answers.

1. Compared to 100 years ago, how much more water do we use now?

    a. about sixty times as much

    b. about six times as much

    c. about sixteen times as much

2. What solution does the video suggest for the world's water problems?

    a. taking more water from rivers

    b. learning how to use ocean water

    c. reducing the demand for water

3. Where did Marie get the information about the numbers of people living in cities?

    a. a report by the United States government

    b. a report from the European Union

    c. a report issued by the United Nations

4. What does Marie say about the population around Lake Chad?

    a. It's decreasing.

    b. It's increasing.

    c. It isn't changing.

5. What do the students say they will do after the discussion?

   a. organize their ideas and information

   b. review all of their data

   c. watch the video again

 D. **IDENTIFY** Work with a partner. Complete the chart with numbers from the box. Use your notes to help you. Then watch and listen again to check your answers.

| 120 | more than 55 | over 300 million trillion | 38 million |
| 29.8 | 8,000 | over one billion | |

1. Gallons of water on Earth	
2. Number of people without clean drinking water	
3. Liters of water needed to produce one cup of coffee	
4. Liters of water needed to produce one hamburger	
5. Percent of world's population living in cities in 1950	
6. Percent of world's population living in cities in 2017	
7. Population living around Lake Chad	

E. **DISCUSS** Work in a group. Take turns asking and answering the questions.

1. One cup of coffee has about one cup of water. One hamburger has one small piece of meat. How can you explain the large amount of water used to produce these things?

2. In the video, the speaker says that water shortages could "lead to wars." Why might this happen?

3. What kinds of solutions do you think the students will suggest for the world's water problems?

iQ PRACTICE Go online for additional listening and comprehension.
Practice > Unit 8 > Activity 4

 ## SAY WHAT YOU THINK

DISCUSS Discuss the questions in a group.

1. Imagine that you don't have enough water for basic things like drinking, cooking, and cleaning. How would this affect you? What could you do about it?

2. Jing and Marie talk about the number of people who die from water-related illnesses like cholera. How can this be prevented?

LISTENING 1   165

LISTENING SKILL Recognizing facts and opinions

A **fact** is something that is true. It can be information about an event, information about a person, or a statistic.

> About two million children under five die every year from water-related illnesses.

An **opinion** is a person's belief or attitude about something. Opinions often have key words like *I think*, *I feel*, or *I'd say*. Most opinions also make value judgments.

> **I think** the lack of clean water is the **most serious** problem in the world today.

Opinions are neither true nor untrue. Opinions can be supported with facts.

> **Opinion:** I think the lack of clean water is the most serious problem in the world today.
>
> **Supporting fact:** The lack of clean water causes the deaths of about two million children under five every year.

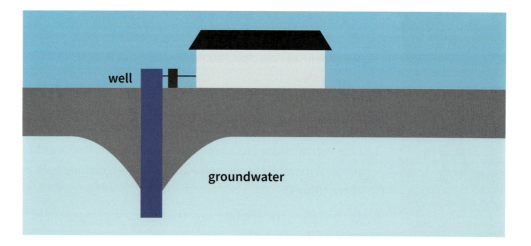

A. CATEGORIZE Listen to these comments from an online discussion about using underground water as a solution to the water problem. Write *fact* or *opinion* for each statement. Write down key words you hear that tell you that each statement is a fact or opinion.

Name	Fact or Opinion	Key Words
Paul	opinion	"seems to me"
Sara		
Liza		
Jamal		
Walaa		
Paul		

B. EVALUATE Work in a group. Compare your responses and notes in the chart in Activity A. If your responses are different, discuss and decide on the correct response. Then listen to the recording again with the group.

iQ PRACTICE Go online for more practice with recognizing facts and opinions. *Practice > Unit 8 > Activity 5*

NOTE-TAKING SKILL Using notes to write a summary

When you review your notes after a class, it can be helpful to write a short summary of the class discussion. Doing this will help you remember the main points. These are a few things to consider when writing a summary.

- Remember that a summary focuses only on the main ideas and does not include a lot of details.

- Notes use single words, short phrases, and many abbreviations. In the summary, you should use complete sentences and write words out fully.

- In a summary, you should try to use your own words to express ideas when possible.

A. EVALUATE Look at one student's notes about the video in Unit 7, *The Nomads of Outer Mongolia*. Then read the summary. Underline three (or more) examples of details that are NOT included in the summary.

A. Where
   Outer Mongolia
   Darhad Valley
   South of Siberia
B. Who?
   Darhad tribe — nomad
   no perm. settle.
C. Lifestyle
   animals / important food clothing
   dangers wolves, bad weather
   herd animals / good pastures
   live in two felt-lined tents "gers"
   gas stove, TV
D. Travel
   Mount. 3,000 m snow
   Wom. make food yogurt cheese
   return spring

The nomads of Outer Mongolia are called the Darhad people. Nomads move from one place to another during the year. Their animals are very important because they give them food and clothing. Bad weather and wolves are dangers they experience. In the winter, they travel over high mountains in the snow. They carry their tents and food with them. They need to find good pastures for their animals. They come back in the spring.

B. SYNTHESIZE Review your notes about the video and class discussion in Listening 1. Write a short summary of the main ideas that the students will include in their report about the importance of clean water.

C. **EXTEND** Work with a partner. Compare your summaries. Did you mention all the main ideas? Did you include any unnecessary details?

iQ PRACTICE Go online for more practice with using notes to write a summary.
Practice > Unit 8 > Activity 6

LISTENING 2 Is It Possible to Be Too Clean?

OBJECTIVE ▶ You are going to listen to a lecture about the connection between cleanliness and the immune system. The immune system in the human body protects us from disease. As you listen, gather information and ideas about the importance of cleanliness.

PREVIEW THE LISTENING

A. **VOCABULARY** Here are some words from Listening 2. Read the definitions. Then complete each sentence with the correct word.

> **allergy** (*noun*) a condition that makes you sick when you eat or touch something that does not normally make people sick
> **automatically** (*adverb*) done by itself; without human control
> **bacteria** (*noun*) ᛙ very tiny living things
> **defense** (*noun*) ᛙ protection of something from an attack
> **digest** (*verb*) to change food in the stomach so it can be used by the body
> **dirt** (*noun*) ᛙ a thing that isn't clean, like dust or mud
> **germs** (*noun*) tiny living things that cause disease
> **old-fashioned** (*adjective*) not modern
> **sensible** (*adjective*) ᛙ having good judgment; being reasonable

ᛙ Oxford 3000™ words   **OPAL** Oxford Phrasal Academic Lexicon

1. Did you know that yogurt is made with two kinds of "good" _____? They turn milk into yogurt. There are thousands in every cup.

2. Let's see, Ashley can't eat chocolate or strawberries. She can't have any pets in the house. And don't ever give her flowers. She has a terrible _____ problem.

3. You don't have to turn off my computer. It will turn off _____ in two hours.

4. Yogurt may not upset your stomach like other milk products. In fact, it helps you _____ your food.

5. I have a special program on my computer as a _____ against viruses that may attack it.

6. Please take your muddy shoes off before you come in the house. I don't want _____ all over my clean floor.

7. Michael decided not to go out tonight because he has an important test tomorrow. That was a(n) _____ decision.

8. I've had this dress for 20 years. It looks extremely _____ now.

9. Please cover your mouth when you cough. You're spreading your _____ all over. I don't want to get sick.

iQ PRACTICE Go online for more practice with the vocabulary.
Practice > Unit 8 > Activities 7–8

B. PREVIEW You are going to listen to a lecture about the connection between cleanliness and the immune system. Work with a partner. Discuss these questions: Is it possible to be too clean? Why or why not?

WORK WITH THE LISTENING

A. LISTEN AND TAKE NOTES Listen to the lecture and take notes. Use the outline to help you.

Is it poss. to be too clean?
A *Change in attitudes re: dirt*
   - *Past*
   - *Present*

B *Studies re: germs*
   - *Germany*
   - *Australia*
C *Conclusion*

B. SYNTHESIZE Use your notes to write a short summary of the lecture. Then compare your notes and summary with a partner.

C. ANALYZE Read the sentences. Choose the answer that best completes each statement. Then listen and check your answers.

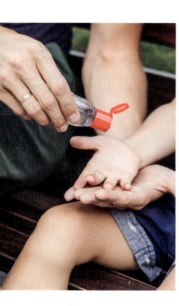

1. According to the speaker, people in the past ____.
   a. were very dirty
   b. were much more worried about cleanliness than we are today
   c. were more relaxed about touching dirt

2. One study showed that children living in an environment with fewer germs ____.
   a. developed fewer allergies
   b. didn't develop strong immune systems
   c. never got sick

3. The speaker says that ____.
   a. some bacteria are good for us
   b. all bacteria cause disease
   c. bacteria are not necessary

D. CATEGORIZE Read the statements. Write *T* (true) or *F* (false). Then correct the false statements.

____ 1. The speaker's grandmother might let her eat cookies that fell on the floor.

____ 2. Carrying hand sanitizer in your pocket is an old-fashioned custom.

____ 3. We should stop taking regular baths and let our houses get dirty.

____ 4. The German study showed that children who lived in cities and had no pets were healthier than kids who lived on farms.

____ 5. In Australia, some people are giving kids "dirt pills" because they think this will help them develop a defense against asthma.

____ 6. Bacteria are necessary in order to create compost from food waste.

E. ANALYZE Listen to the sentences from the lecture. Choose the sentence closest in meaning to the sentence you hear.

1. a. Dirt, germs, and bacteria are harmful to our immune systems.
   b. People nowadays spend too much time cleaning and bathing.
   c. A little contact with dirt and germs helps build our defense against disease.

2. a. Some Australian children with asthma are taking "dirt" pills. The pills have bacteria the children did not come into contact with as babies.
   b. In Australia, more children are getting asthma because they touched the bacteria that cause the disease when they were babies.
   c. In Australia, little babies are taking "dirt pills" so they won't get asthma.

3. a. People should all be a lot dirtier.
   b. Some people today are a little bit too clean.
   c. Some people today are too dirty.

F. EXPLAIN Do hand sanitizers work? Work in a group. Read the explanation and study the charts. Then answer the questions.

A group of doctors did a study in an elementary school. They gave hand sanitizers to the students in some classrooms (Group A), but not in others (Group B). Then they counted the number of days students were absent because of illness, either stomach illnesses or colds. The study continued for eight weeks.

Absences for stomach illnesses

	0	1	2	3	Total days absent
Group A	123	15	6	2	33
Group B	105	21	9	3	48

Absences for colds

	0	1	2	3	Total days absent
Group A	106	22	10	3	51
Group B	104	19	10	5	54

1. Which group had more days absent because of stomach illnesses?
2. Which group had more days absent because of colds?
3. How are the results for stomach illnesses and colds different?
4. Do you think that this study proves that hand sanitizers help keep children healthier?

SAY WHAT YOU THINK

SYNTHESIZE Think about Listening 1 and Listening 2 as you discuss the questions.

1. Before Listening 2, you discussed the question "Is it possible to be too clean?" How did you answer this question before listening? What is your answer now? Did it change? Why or why not?

2. Do you worry about contact with germs? Why or why not?

3. As countries around the world become more modern, the demand for water will grow. What can people do about this?

4. Imagine that someone advised you to "let your children play in the dirt." How would you reply?

VOCABULARY SKILL Using the dictionary

Dictionaries have many different kinds of information about words. In addition to the meaning of the word, a dictionary entry includes:

- part of speech—for example, *noun, verb, adjective*
- word forms, such as plurals, past tense, and participle forms, and comparatives
- pronunciation
- grammatical information about words—for example, countability of nouns [C for *countable*, U for *uncountable*]

An entry can also include:

- some synonyms or antonyms (opposites)
- example phrases and sentences

TIP FOR SUCCESS

When possible, use an English learner's dictionary. It gives simple definitions and examples of words.

A. IDENTIFY Read the dictionary entry for the word *disease*. Then mark the different kinds of information.

1. Circle the pronunciation information.
2. Underline the part of speech.
3. Put a check (✓) above the grammar information.
4. Put a star (★) next to the example sentences or phrases.

> **dis·ease** /dɪˈziz/ *noun* [C, U] (**HEALTH**) an illness of the body in humans, animals, or plants: *an infectious disease* ♦ *Rats and flies spread disease.* ▶ **diseased** *adj.*: *His diseased kidney had to be removed.*

All dictionary entries adapted from the *Oxford American Dictionary for learners of English* © Oxford University Press 2011.

B. INVESTIGATE Use a dictionary to answer the questions about the bold words. Sometimes you may need to look at words before or after the bold word to find the answer.

1. Is the word **bacteria** singular or plural? _____

2. What's an adjective in the same word family as the noun **sanitation**?
   _____

3. What's the verb in the same word family as the noun **defense**?
   _____

4. What's the adverb form of the adjective **sensible**? _____

5. In Listening 2, the speaker says, "No one is saying that we should stop **bathing**." How do you spell the base form of the verb **bathing**?
   _____

6. Do you pronounce the *th* in **asthma**? _____

C. ANALYZE Read the sentences. Identify the error in each sentence. Then rewrite each sentence to correct the error.

1. Some bacteria doesn't make you sick.
   <u>Some bacteria don't make you sick.</u>

2. The kitchen in that restaurant is not sanitation.
   _____

3. Don't worry about me! I can defense myself if there's a problem.
   _____

4. After that big storm, I think it's very sensibly to start boiling our drinking water.
   _____

5. My sister baths her baby before bed. The warm water relaxes him.
   _____

6. We can't have a cat because my son has asma.
   _____

iQ PRACTICE Go online for more practice using the dictionary.
Practice > Unit 8 > Activity 9

SPEAKING

OBJECTIVE ▶ At the end of this unit, you are going to participate in a group discussion about a problem related to water and sanitation. You will present a solution to the problem and try to persuade others that your solution is the best one.

GRAMMAR *If* clauses for future possibility

If **clauses** can express future possibility. Sentences with *if* clauses show a cause-and-effect relationship. The *if* clause describes the cause. The result clause gives a possible effect.

The verb in the *if* clause is in the simple present. The result clause uses a modal, such as **will**, **can**, or **may/might** + **verb**. The choice depends on how certain the speaker is about the result.

if clause	result clause
If there **is** a lack of clean water,	diseases **will spread** very quickly.
If you **use** hand sanitizer,	you **might not get** sick this winter.

Note: The *if* clause and the result clause can come in either order. When the *if* clause is first, it is followed by a comma. There's no comma when the result clause is first.

☐ Diseases will spread very quickly if there is a lack of clean water.

iQ RESOURCES Go online to watch the Grammar Skill Video.
Resources > Video > Unit 8 > Grammar Skill Video

A. CATEGORIZE Listen to the sentences. Write the cause and the effect in each sentence.

	Cause	Effect
1	test the water	find out it's polluted
2		
3		
4		
5		

174 UNIT 8 How important is cleanliness?

B. COMPOSE Look at the words and phrases below. Use the words and phrases to write sentences with *if* clauses.

1. they / use the underground water source / have water for 400 years

   _____

2. I / use hand sanitizer / might not get sick

   _____

3. we / not get rain / crops / die

   _____

4. Sarah / save more water / take shorter showers

   _____

5. people / have clean water / be fewer deaths

   _____

6. John / spread germs / not wash his hands

   _____

C. EVALUATE Compare your sentences with a partner. Take turns saying your sentences.

iQ PRACTICE Go online for more practice with *if* clauses for future possibility. *Practice > Unit 8 > Activity 10*

iQ PRACTICE Go online for the Grammar Expansion: future time clauses. *Practice > Unit 8 > Activity 11*

PRONUNCIATION Function words and stress

Function words are the short words that connect the content words in a sentence. Function words are usually not stressed. They are also pronounced more quickly than content words. They can include words like these.

articles: *the, a, an*	**forms of the verbs** *be, do,* or *have*
pronouns: *he, she, it*	**conjunctions:** *and, but, or*
prepositions: *in, on, at, for*	**modals** such as *can* or *will*

The bold words in this sentence are function words.

People use special soaps **that** kill germs, **and** they carry hand sanitizers **in their** pockets.

A. IDENTIFY Read the paragraph. Underline the function words. Then listen and focus on the pronunciation of the function words.

TIP FOR SUCCESS

Most of us do not hear every word when we listen. We know which words are there because we know the language. We don't need to hear them.

> There is no new water on Earth. All of the water on Earth—the rivers, lakes, oceans, ice at the North and South Poles, clouds, and rain—is about one billion years old. The water moves around the planet. It can change to ice, to rain, or to fog, but it's always the same water. Think about it. The population of the world is growing, but the supply of water is always the same.

B. APPLY Work with a partner. Take turns reading the paragraph in Activity A. Make sure you stress the content words and not the function words.

 C. APPLY Some of the function words in this paragraph are missing. Listen and write the missing function words.

"Water, water, everywhere, nor any drop to drink." Those _____*are*_____ the words _____ the famous English
                                                              1   2
poet Samuel Coleridge. He was writing about _____ man
                                                                        3
alone _____ a boat on _____ ocean. The words
           4   5
might also describe _____ condition _____
                                       6   7
the people _____ our planet. Earth has about 1.4 billion cubic
                      8

kilometers _____9_____ water. The problem _____10_____ that 97.5 percent _____11_____ that water is salt water in the oceans _____12_____ the seas. Only 2.5 percent is fresh water. Most _____13_____ that fresh water _____14_____ in the ice at the North _____15_____ South Poles or underground. Only 0.3 percent of _____16_____ fresh water is in lakes _____17_____ rivers where people _____18_____ easily find and use _____19_____.

D. APPLY Practice reading the paragraph in Activity C with a partner.

iQ PRACTICE Go online for more practice with function words and stress. *Practice > Unit 8 > Activity 12*

CRITICAL THINKING STRATEGY

Appraising solutions to problems

When you listen to other people suggest solutions to a problem, you need to **appraise** what they are saying. To appraise means to analyze, assess, and make a judgment about their solutions. You might then decide whether you agree or disagree. You might also decide that you need more information.

iQ PRACTICE Go online to watch the Critical Thinking Video and check your comprehension. *Practice > Unit 8 > Activity 13*

E. INVESTIGATE Read the case study below. What problem does it describe? Discuss with a partner.

> There is a beautiful, clean river that comes down from the mountains. There are several villages on the banks of the river, and the people use the water for washing, cooking, and drinking. The problem is that some of the farmers in this area bring their animals down to the river to drink. This means that the animal waste gets into the water and pollutes it. The water is no longer safe. People who live near the river want the farmers to stop using the river for the animals.

F. EVALUATE Read the solutions some people have suggested. Appraise each statement. Mark each as *A* (agree), *D* (disagree) or *N* (need more information), depending on what you decide for each.

____ 1. Residents should build fences along the river to prevent animals from getting to the water.

____ 2. Residents should meet with the farmers to discuss the problem.

____ 3. Residents should look for other ways to bring water to the animals. For example, they could build a system that brings water from the river to where the animals are.

____ 4. Residents should ask the government to dig a community well, away from the river. This water would be for people, so they don't need to use the river water. Then the farmers could continue to take their animals to the river.

____ 5. Residents should have the water tested, so they know exactly what the problems are with the water quality.

G. EXPLAIN Work with a group. Compare and discuss your answers. Give reasons to support your opinions. If you need more information for some solutions, what questions would you ask?

SPEAKING SKILL Participating in a group discussion

Participating in a group discussion can be challenging for a language learner. Here are a few suggestions to help you.

- Listen carefully to what others are saying. Listen for the topic of the discussion and the main ideas.
- When you speak, start by referring to something the previous speaker said. Make sure your comment relates to the topic.
- Speak clearly and be sure to speak loudly enough for people to hear you.
- Don't interrupt people. Wait for a break in the conversation before you speak.
- Help others participate by asking questions and saying things like, "Mary, we haven't heard your ideas yet."

A. DISCUSS Listen to parts of the conversation in Listening 1. Discuss the questions with a partner.

Part 1

1. How does Jing invite Marie to participate in the conversation?
2. How do you know that Marie was listening to what Jing said?

Part 2

3. What's the problem with Toby's comment about being too clean?
4. What does Emma say to Toby? How does this help the conversation?

Part 3

5. How does Marie speak at the start—very softly or firmly and clearly? Is this a problem? Why or why not?
6. What does Jing do to Marie?
7. What does Emma do about it?
8. What does Jing say at the end?

B. CREATE Work in a group. Choose one of the following topics or use your own idea. Talk about it for five minutes. During that time, everyone in the group should speak at least once. Use the suggestions in the Speaking Skill box.

Three things we can do now to save water
Two things we can do to make our city cleaner
What we should teach children about cleanliness

iQ PRACTICE Go online for more practice with participating in a group discussion. *Practice > Unit 8 > Activity 14*

UNIT ASSIGNMENT Give a persuasive presentation

OBJECTIVE ▶ In this section, you are going to give a persuasive presentation. As you prepare your presentation, think about the Unit Question, "How important is cleanliness?" Use information from Listening 1, Listening 2, and your work in this unit to support your presentation. Refer to the Self-Assessment checklist on page 182.

CONSIDER THE IDEAS

INVESTIGATE With a partner, read the case studies about issues related to water and sanitation. For each case, discuss the questions.

1. What problem does the case present?
2. Who are the people involved?
3. How do the people agree or disagree about the situation?

Case 1

A city has a serious problem with its water supply. For several years there has been very little rain. The lake that supplies the city with water is getting smaller and smaller. The city officials are telling people that they have to use less water. But most people don't seem to understand this. They don't want to change the way they use water. One official says, "If people won't change, we will soon have to start rationing water. That means that we would give people only a small amount of water each day. No one will like that!"

Case 2

The principal and a group of teachers at a high school want to provide hand sanitizer in the classrooms. They think that if teachers and students use these frequently, fewer people will get sick from colds and flu. Many parents and some teachers are against this idea. They say that this is taking cleanliness too far. They say hand sanitizers are not a substitute for soap and water. They say the best way to keep your hands clean is to wash them for at least 15 seconds with warm water and soap. They point out that the bathrooms at the school are often out of soap. They're telling the principal, "Buy more soap, not hand sanitizer!"

PREPARE AND SPEAK

TIP FOR SUCCESS

As you participate in these activities, try to follow the suggestions for participating in group discussions.

A. GATHER IDEAS Work in a group. Choose one of the cases in the Consider the Ideas section. Then follow these steps. Use the chart to help you organize your ideas.

1. Review the case and make sure everyone understands the problem.
2. Brainstorm possible solutions for the problem.
3. For each solution, think of any pros (advantages) or cons (disadvantages) there might be. What will the people involved think of the solution? Will they accept it?

Case Study: _____

Solutions	Pros and Cons
1.	Pro:
	Con:
2.	Pro:
	Con:
3.	Pro:
	Con:

B. ORGANIZE IDEAS As a group, prepare a presentation of the case you picked and the best solutions. Each person in the group should be responsible for one possible solution. During the presentation, you will try to persuade your audience that your solution is best.

C. SPEAK Present your case and the solutions to the class. After the presentation, discuss these questions with the class. Refer to the Self-Assessment checklist below before you begin.

1. Ask the class, "Did you agree or disagree with our solutions? Why or why not?"

2. What other solutions can you think of for this case?

iQ PRACTICE Go online for your alternate Unit Assignment.
Practice > Unit 8 > Activity 15

CHECK AND REFLECT

A. CHECK Think about the Unit Assignment as you complete the Self-Assessment checklist.

SELF-ASSESSMENT	Yes	No
I was able to speak easily about the topic.	☐	☐
My partner, group, and class understood me.	☐	☐
I used *if* clauses for future possibility.	☐	☐
I used vocabulary from the unit.	☐	☐
I participated in a group discussion.	☐	☐
I used correct stress for function words.	☐	☐

B. REFLECT Discuss these questions with a partner or group.

1. What is something new you learned in this unit?

2. Look back at the Unit Question—How important is cleanliness? Is your answer different now than when you started this unit? If yes, how is it different? Why?

iQ PRACTICE Go to the online discussion board to discuss the questions.
Practice > Unit 8 > Activity 16

TRACK YOUR SUCCESS

iQ PRACTICE Go online to check the words and phrases you have learned in this unit. *Practice > Unit 8 > Activity 17*

Check (✓) the skills and strategies you learned. If you need more work on a skill, refer to the page(s) in parentheses.

LISTENING	☐ I can recognize facts and opinions. (p. 166)
NOTE-TAKING	☐ I can use notes to write a summary. (p. 167)
VOCABULARY	☐ I can use the dictionary to find information about words. (p. 172)
GRAMMAR	☐ I can use *if* clauses for future possibility. (p. 174)
PRONUNCIATION	☐ I can stress function words properly. (p. 175)
CRITICAL THINKING	☐ I can appraise solutions to a problem. (p. 177)
SPEAKING	☐ I can participate in a group discussion. (p. 179)
OBJECTIVE ▶	☐ I can gather information and ideas to participate in a discussion about the importance of clean water.

VOCABULARY LIST AND CEFR CORRELATION

🔑 The **Oxford 3000**™ is a list of the 3,000 core words that every learner of English needs to know. The words have been chosen based on their frequency in the Oxford English Corpus and relevance to learners of English. Every word is aligned to the CEFR, guiding learners on the words they should know at the A1–B2 level.

OPAL The **Oxford Phrasal Academic Lexicon** is an essential guide to the most important words and phrases to know for academic English. The word lists are based on the Oxford Corpus of Academic English and the British Academic Spoken English corpus.

The **Common European Framework of Reference for Language (CEFR)** provides a basic description of what language learners have to do to use language effectively. The system contains 6 reference levels: A1, A2, B1, B2, C1, C2.

UNIT 1

advertise *(v.)* 🔑 A2
affordable *(adj.)* B2
brake *(n.)*
buck the trend *(v. phr.)*
chat *(v.)* 🔑 A2
decline *(v.)* 🔑 OPAL B2
enormous *(adj.)* 🔑 A2
essential *(adj.)* 🔑 OPAL B1
failure *(n.)* 🔑 OPAL B2
get the point *(v. phr.)*
postage *(n.)*
potential *(adj.)* 🔑 OPAL B2
realize *(v.)* 🔑 A2
reasonable *(adj.)* 🔑 OPAL B2
wealthy *(adj.)* 🔑 B2
wheel *(n.)* 🔑 A2

UNIT 2

beautiful *(adj.)* 🔑 A1
blend in *(v. phr.)*
brilliant *(adj.)* 🔑 A2
hide *(v.)* 🔑 A2
insect *(n.)* 🔑 A2
match *(v.)* 🔑 B1
peaceful *(adj.)* 🔑 B1
poison *(n.)* 🔑 B1
predator *(n.)* C1
pride *(n.)* B2
shape *(n.)* 🔑 OPAL A2
skin *(n.)* 🔑 A2
solid *(adj.)* 🔑 B1
straight *(adj.)* 🔑 A2
survive *(v.)* 🔑 B1
warning *(n.)* 🔑 B1
wing *(n.)* 🔑 B1

UNIT 3

admit *(v.)* 🔑 B1
attentive *(adj.)*
behavior *(n.)* 🔑 OPAL A2
courteous *(adj.)*
courtesy *(n.)* C1
deal with *(v. phr.)* A2
etiquette *(n.)*
improve *(v.)* 🔑 OPAL A1
increase *(n.)* 🔑 OPAL A2
influence *(n.)* 🔑 OPAL B1
manners *(n.)* 🔑 A2
polite *(adj.)* 🔑 A2
principal *(n.)* B2
respect *(n.)* 🔑 OPAL B1
rude *(adj.)* 🔑 A2
scream *(v.)* 🔑 B2
shout out *(v. phr.)*
society *(n.)* 🔑 OPAL A2
valuable *(adj.)* 🔑 OPAL B1
violence *(n.)* 🔑 OPAL B2

UNIT 4

common *(adj.)* 🔑 OPAL A1
dependent on *(adj. phr.)* OPAL B2
digital *(adj.)* OPAL 🔑 A2
disconnect *(v.)*
face-to-face *(adj. phr. / adv. phr.)*
find *(v.)* OPAL 🔑 B1
forever *(adv.)* 🔑 B2
friendship *(n.)* 🔑 B1
headline *(n.)* 🔑 B1
meaningful *(adj.)* OPAL C1
post *(v.)* 🔑 A1
privacy *(n.)* 🔑 B2
relationship *(n.)* 🔑 OPAL A2
scary *(adj.)* 🔑 A2
silly *(adj.)* 🔑 B1
strange *(adj.)* 🔑 A2

UNIT 5

ancestor *(n.)* B2
appearance *(n.)* 🔑 A2
coincidence *(n.)* B2
cousin *(n.)* 🔑 A1
database *(n.)* B2
get along *(v. phr.)*
identity *(n.)* 🔑 OPAL B1
inherit *(v.)* B2
input *(n.)* OPAL B2
participant *(n.)* 🔑 OPAL B2
record *(n.)* 🔑 OPAL A2
search *(v.)* 🔑 A2
separate *(adj.)* 🔑 OPAL A2
slave *(n.)* 🔑 B2
tendency *(n.)* OPAL B2
twin *(n.)* 🔑 A2

UNIT 6

apply *(v.)* 🔑 OPAL B2
benefit *(n.)* 🔑 OPAL A2
coach *(n.)* 🔑 A2
competitive *(adj.)* 🔑 B1
developer *(n.)*
disappointment *(n.)* B2
entertainment *(n.)* 🔑 B1
lose *(v.)* 🔑 A1

object *(n.)* 🔑 OPAL B2
positive *(adj.)* 🔑 OPAL A1
pressure *(n.)* 🔑 OPAL B1
react *(v.)* 🔑 OPAL A2
stress *(n.)* 🔑 OPAL A2
tournament *(n.)* B2
useful *(adj.)* 🔑 OPAL A1
wonderful *(adj.)* 🔑 A1

UNIT 7

attack *(v.)* 🔑 OPAL A2
earthquake *(n.)* 🔑 B1
elevator *(n.)*
fascinating *(adj.)* 🔑 B1
freezing *(adj.)*
height *(n.)* 🔑 A2
neighborhood *(n.)* 🔑 B1
permanent *(adj.)* 🔑 B2
process *(v.)* 🔑 OPAL B2
remain *(v.)* 🔑 B1
resident *(n.)* 🔑 OPAL B2
response *(n.)* 🔑 OPAL A2
shake *(v.)* 🔑 A2
suburb *(n.)* B2
suitable *(adj.)* 🔑 OPAL B1
threat *(n.)* 🔑 OPAL B2

UNIT 8

agriculture *(n.)* B2
allergy *(n.)*
automatically *(adv.)* B2
bacteria *(n.)* 🔑 B2
climate *(n.)* 🔑 OPAL A2
consequence *(n.)* 🔑 OPAL B1
defense *(n.)* 🔑 B2
demand *(n.)* 🔑 OPAL B2
digest *(v.)*
dirt *(n.)* 🔑 B1
disease *(n.)* 🔑 A2
germs *(n.)*
grow *(v.)* 🔑 OPAL A1
lack of *(n. phr.)*
old-fashioned *(adj.)* 🔑 B1
prevent *(v.)* 🔑 OPAL A2
sensible *(adj.)* 🔑 B1
shortage *(n.)* B2
supply *(n.)* 🔑 OPAL B1